ADVANCED PRAISE FOR

Prayers for You

I am greatly inspired by Shireen Spencer's collection of prayers. For the past two years, I have looked forward to reading her daily prayers as she seems to know exactly what we are facing through life's challenges. It is my pleasure to share Shireen's prayers with others globally, to help lift their spirits. When our faith is challenged, reading these inspiring words can deepen our understanding of someone larger than life—God. Our faith is the most powerful thing we have and our confidence in life comes through our convictions after life-threatening diseases and any struggle. These daily prayers uplift our spirits and give us a reason to hope.

—Leila Springer
Founder/President /CEO of The Olive Branch of Hope
Cancer Support Care

Shireen Spencer writes and speaks from a place of confident trust in the Lord. I have known her for many years and she remains consistent in her faith. When you read Shireen's prayers and pray with her you are connecting with a woman who has a heart after her God. This is what God desires from all of us.

—Rev. Patricia Russell
Recording Artist, Speaker, Author, Coach

Whether you have the privilege of reading one or many of Shireen Spencer's stunningly written prayers, you will know you have experienced the words of someone who has found deep joy and inspiration in God's presence. Shireen's prayers are a revelation of the good, kind, and unchanging nature of a loving God who has an ear always to the prayers of His children. Shireen's prayers encourage us all to lean into the wide and deep stream of a dialogue with God that will leave us richer and more tethered in our faith. I highly recommend Shireen's prayers to you and know you will experience transformation in your prayer life with God.

—Cathie Ostapchuk
Founder and Lead of Gather Women
Author of *Brave Women, Bold Moves*

Prayers
FOR YOU

365 Days of Heartfelt
Prayers and Meditations

SHIREEN SPENCER

PRAYERS FOR YOU
Copyright © 2022 by Shireen Spencer

ISBN: 978-1-4866-2241-2
eBook ISBN: 978-1-4866-2242-9

Printed in Canada

Word Alive Press
119 De Baets Street Winnipeg, MB R2J 3R9
www.wordalivepress.ca

WORD ALIVE
—P R E S S—

MIX
Paper from
responsible sources
FSC   FSC® C103567
www.fsc.org

Cataloguing in Publication information can be obtained from Library and Archives Canada.

DEDICATION

I dedicate this book to Che and Micah, my two precious sons. I have always had great examples of prayer warriors in my life, and my prayer is that you will learn from me the importance and value of prayer. My heart's desire is that you will both see God do amazing things in you and through you as you make prayer a priority in your lives.

INTRODUCTION

I have always loved praying. I think this is a gift God has blessed me with throughout my life. I've been blessed with great role models and mentors who have taught me the importance of prayer, persistence in prayer, power in prayer, and the love of prayer. They taught me the value of praying scripture and being able to see that God keep His Word and promises. I truly see prayer as my lifeline. I've never been able to keep this joy of praying to myself, and I'm glad that I haven't.

I started out writing these prayers as an act of obedience and a gift of encouragement to a few women's groups I was privileged to minister with. It was because of these precious women that I wrote a year's worth of prayers and decided to compile them. As I shared my prayers, the women shared them with many others, and I received numerous messages from strangers telling me that God met them and spoke exactly what they needed at the right time.

God wants His children to feel comfortable sharing their hearts with Him and having Him share His heart with them. Prayer allows this exchange to happen. The body of Christ needs to be strengthened, and ·our strength comes from knowing that God's Word is life to us. These prayers are all founded and grounded in scripture. Praying scripture reminds us of who God is and who we are in Christ. I don't want to forget, and I don't want you to forget it either. On these pages are heartfelt prayers that I pray for myself as much as I pray for you.

While this is a book of prayer, it's also a study in scripture to feed your prayers with God's truth. Read the prayers and let's pray together but also take time in the Word. God's Word does not return to Him void. It transforms our lives and circumstances. I have included the scriptures my prayers came from at the beginning of each entry. May the Lord direct your heart to which ones He wants you to meditate on, and may they lead you to pray your own scripture prayers that will build your life and bring God-given answers. May your prayer journey this year draw you closer to God every day. I will be praying with you and for you.

At the end of each prayer please reflect and use the provided scriptures to write your own prayer if you feel led. Here are two questions to help you:

1. What message is God speaking to you through his scriptures today?

2. Write his message down. Write your own prayer.

Prayers
FOR YOU

365 Days of Heartfelt
Prayers and Meditations

1

Keep Your Eyes on God

Matthew 21:21; Isaiah 40:4; Zechariah 4:6–10;
Proverbs 15:3; Psalm 32:8; Habakkuk 3:19; Isaiah 26:7

May you pray today with your eyes on the one who can move mountains. May you continue to look up so that you can make it over. May your focus be moved from difficulty to destination by moving your attention to the one who is greater than anything and can handle everything. You cannot see the answers to prayer by looking at your obstacles.

May God's gaze on you be noticed by you. May you look at God and see how much love, strength, and provision is being extended to you. Prayer brings God's presence closer and takes you farther than you thought you could go. Keep your eyes on Him and He will take you to higher ground and onto straighter paths.

2

May You See Growth

Psalm 37:5, 125:5–6; 2 Corinthians 9:6–11; Proverbs 10:22, 16:3

May the things you have worked so hard for begin to have life today. May the seeds you have planted and watered with tears begin to grow as the Son shines on them. May you begin to reap a harvest as God brings your increase and accelerates your breakthrough.

May "struggle" be a word of the past, "strength" be the word of your present, and "success" be the word that makes its home in your future. May you be anointed with favour and blessing as you move forward in the plans God has for you. May you stay committed to God and walk boldly and confidently as God acts on your behalf.

3

You Are Stronger

Zechariah 4:6; Exodus 15:2; Isaiah 41:10, 29; Proverbs 24:16;
2 Corinthians 4:9; 16–18; Psalm 34:27; 1 Chronicles 29:11

May you know that you are stronger than you think. May you know that the reason for your strength is Jesus, and He is alive and well. May you know that as you take the Holy Spirit as your companion, you will walk in resilience. You will bounce back. You will get up again.

May you know that God is renewing you and strengthening you from the inside. May you feel the strength of God's hand upholding you. May you know that there is never a moment of weakness in the great God you serve. He is always strong. You can trust Him. Greatness, power, glory, victory, and majesty are God.

4

Fruit of Discipline

Hebrews 12:6, 11; Revelation 3:19; Proverbs 3:11–12, 6:23, 12:1;
Job 5:17

May you experience the fruit of discipline today. May peace and righteousness grow in you as the choice of discipline trains you to be the better you. May you grow in knowledge of the Lord and who He has called you to be as you accept the love of God through discipline in your life.

May you know that the Lord delights in you and is building strength and character that will open many doors for you. May you know that as you walk in discipline, you are walking the way of life. You will experience freedom. You will add vitality to your life. Your way will be bright. May you find the blessings in living a life of discipline. The Lord loves you.

5

Run Your Race

Hebrews 12:1; 2 Timothy 4:7; Philippians 3:13–14; Galatians 6:9

As you run your race today, may your life and choices encourage others to run theirs in purity, confidence, and with endurance. May you push yourself and others to win. There's a prize for all who finish the race well. May you know that you have a cloud of witnesses cheering you on. Don't give up. Keep going. As you go, cheer loudly for others. May you help others along the way to complete their journey. May you be an encourager, helper, and supporter who strengthens others in their time of weakness. May you know that there is enough room to celebrate everyone's victory and celebrate many times.

6

May You Love Obedience

1 John 5:2–4; Acts 5:29; Isaiah 1:19

May your love for God be shown by your walk of obedience. May you give ear to His directions with intention. May you choose His way on purpose. May obedience to God be more important and of greater value than making others happy. May your heart be moved by what moves God. May you know that in your willingness to make this simple but challenging choice, God has great blessings in store for you.

7

Seek with All Your Heart

Psalm 42, 27:4, 63:1

May you seek after God with all your heart today and see His beauty. May you earnestly seek after Him and let the refreshment of His presence be enough. May your soul long for more of Him, and may nothing take the place of Jesus. May He be your heart's desire—to love the most and to be loved by the most. May you long to worship Him with everything in you.

8

Walk in the Way

Proverbs 13:4, 22:6; Psalm 94:12–14; 1 Timothy 1:7;
1 Corinthians 9:27

May the training you received as a child lead you in the way you should go today. May your days be filled with freedom and rest from trouble. May you know that any discipline the Lord gives comes from a heart of love for you. He will not forsake you but will work on you, with you, and for you until His plan is accomplished.

God has given you a spirit of power, love, and discipline. May you know that you have what it takes to set goals and accomplish them. May your diligence bring you abundance and make you qualified for all that God wants to do in your life.

9

Make the Most of Opportunity

Ephesians 5:15–16; Proverbs 20:13; Galatians 5:22–24; John 15:2–6

May you carefully consider your ways. May you use your time wisely and make the most of every opportunity. May you open your eyes every day to see the gifts of life that God has blessed you with in each moment. May you live with purpose and direction.

Nothing can hold you back or restrict you from living a fruitful life. May you let the Holy Spirt complete His work in you. May you allow pruning to take place to leave room for beautiful growth. May you discipline yourself to spend time in prayer, in the Word, and listening to God's voice. You can do nothing apart from God. May the best use of your time today be spent abiding in Him.

10

Know God Keeps His Promises

Psalm 107:20; Isaiah 53:5; Jeremiah17:14, 30:7; Exodus 23:25;
1 Thessalonians 5:23

May you know that God promises healing. The one you praise is worthy and keeps His promises. May you know that healing is a journey. Do not give up but lean on God and expect Him to complete what He has started.

May you take the time to spend time with Jesus as He works in you, through you, and for you. May you trust God to restore health to you and bring wholeness to your mind, heart, and body. May you experience the peace of God doing a complete work in you.

11

Choose the Way of Faithfulness

Exodus 23:22; Psalm 119:30; 2 Kings 18:6; Luke 11:28

May you see God stand for you against all those who oppose you as you choose to obey Him. May you choose the way of faithfulness to God because you are certain you will find Him walking with you along the way. May you hold fast to the Lord and not depart from following Him as you live out what you have been taught. May you continue to hear the Word of God and do what it says. You are promised blessing as you stay the course.

12

Know the Lord Is God

Deuteronomy 7:9

May you know that in every moment of every day, the Lord your God is God. May you know in every situation you encounter that the Lord your God is God. May you know that wherever you go, the Lord your God is God.

May you know beyond any doubt that God is faithful. May you experience in your today the unfolding of God's promises and covenant made long ago. God's mercies toward you travel through thousands of generations. He loves you.

13

Obey Because You Love

Jeremiah 7:23; Psalm 112:1, 143:10; Exodus 19:5

May you walk in the way God commands because you love Him. May your actions speak louder than words. May all be well with you, just as God promised, as you walk in the way He leads. May you enjoy pleasing God and experience delight in following Him. May you know how much God treasures you, and the blessings He desires to give you for walking in obedience. He will lead you on level ground. He is good and can only lead by His good spirit. May you follow Him confidently.

14

Be a Living Sacrifice

Colossians 3:23; 1 Corinthians 10:31; Romans 12:1; Philippians 4:13

May everything you do today be wrapped in your love and passion for God. May God be glorified because you have offered yourself to Him as a living sacrifice that He can use to make a difference in His world. May you believe that all He has called you to do can be accomplished because His strength resides in you. May you rise in faith as you experience a strength that you know doesn't come from you. May you trust Him more.

15

Keep Following His Lead

John 15:10; Psalm 119:59; Deuteronomy 6:18

May keeping God's commandments be the choice you make to keep you abiding in His love. When you think about which direction to go, may your feet follow the testimonies of God. He is faithful. He has led well before, so you can trust that He will continue to do so. May you continue to do what is right before God. You will walk in wellness and wholeness. As you walk in obedience, may you walk out the fulfillment of God's promises. The Lord will lead you to take possession of all He has promised you. May you know the truth God has shared with you and walk in blessing as you follow Him.

16

Let God Be God

Psalm 61:2–4, 91:1–2, 100:3; John 14:6; Isaiah 40:31; Proverbs 3:5–6

May you let the same God who saved you keep sheltering, sustaining, and shielding you today. May you continue to hold on to His hand, listen to His voice, and follow His direction. May you wait with expectancy on the Lord. You will grow stronger, and He will lead the way. May you know that you will go farther and move with greater clarity waiting on the Lord. Let Him pave the way for you with His footprints. He is the Good Shepherd. He lives to lead and protect you. May you live to follow and stay under His covering. Stay safe in Him.

17

Blessed Obedience

Deuteronomy 4:39–40, 28:1–14; John 13:17; 1 John 2:17

May you experience the life that obedience to God promises you today. May you know that your choices today leave blessings for generations to come. May you know what God asks of you and do it with all your heart. May you be a testimony for all to see of the blessing God has given you and made you to be.

The world and its ways will pass away, but may you hold on to the promise of everlasting life. May it fuel and strengthen your walk of obedience as you look to your future. May you know that the Lord has more blessings than you can contain as you walk confidently in obedience to Him.

18

Never Be Lost

Psalm 25:5, 66:17–20, 145:18–19; Lamentations 3:25; Hebrews 4:16;
Proverbs 8:27; Isaiah 30:18, 21, 40:29, 65:24

May you talk with God today and know that not one breath lifted to Him was lost or wasted. May you walk with God and know that no strength was lost—yours when you held His hand, or His when He carried you. May you wait on God and know that time was not lost but found. Waiting on God redeems the time.

May you trust God in all things and know that you will always find your way. You will never be lost with Him as your compass. He leads you in the way that lasts, produces fruit, and leaves you with joy.

19

Look to Jesus

Matthew 5:8; Psalm 33:4, 34:5; 1 Corinthians 2:10–15;
Luke 6:18, 8:46

A s you look to Jesus today, may you look for Him at work in your life. Those who look to Him are radiant! As you look, may you clearly see. Look to Him with a pure heart. May you get to Jesus today. Do everything in your power, and He will do everything in His.

As you come to Jesus, may you realize all that you will receive. You are blessed to be healed, comforted, safe, and heard. You will receive forgiveness that only He can give, and all the love He has in store for you to free you. The Lord has promised all this and more. His Word is upright, and all He does He does in faithfulness.

20

Embrace the New

Lamentations 3:22–24; Isaiah 42:9; Revelation 21:5; Romans 11:36

May this new day bring an awareness of the new strength, new mercy, new compassion, new opportunities, and new beginnings God is giving to you. May you take hold of new promises. May God bring you a new Word that confirms truth again in your heart and life.

May "new" be accepted and invited. May "new" not be feared but embraced with excitement and expectation. God is always in control. God is in everything. There is nothing "new" to Him. All things come from Him, and He will help you. May you become a "new" person walking in greater faith, hope, belief, and love. May you celebrate the "new" you today.

21

The Earth Is Filled with His Glory

Habakkuk 2:14; 1 Corinthians 10:26

May this day open our eyes to your greatness. May we see the beauty in the sun, the clouds, the earth, and all of creation that speaks to your miracle-working power. May we see you in the faces of those we look at and marvel at how we are all made in your image. Help us, Lord, to be drawn into praise because of your greatness revealed in all that you have created. The earth is yours. We are yours. May we praise you and give you glory. May the knowledge of the glory of God cause us to humbly bow before you in worship. You deserve the honour and the glory.

22

Let God Search You

*Psalm 103:17, 139:23–24; 2 Thessalonians 3:16; Jeremiah 31:3;
Isaiah 26:4, 40:28; 1 John 2:25*

May you give God permission to search your heart today. May you trust Him to show you what needs His touch. He loves you and wants the best for you. May you let Him reveal to you what doesn't please Him. May you allow Him to remove any wicked way so that He can lead you in the way everlasting.

He promises everlasting peace. Receive it. He promises love everlasting. Let nothing distort, hide, or remove that gift. He promises His everlasting presence. Keep Him close. He is patient with you. He is faithful. He has promised life everlasting. May you live in joy because you know your future is guaranteed. May you stand firm in your position of victory. He is your everlasting rock.

23

Let Joy Be Contagious

Proverbs 10:28, 27:17; 1 Chronicles 16:27; Psalm 4:7, 63:6–7

May your joy be contagious today. May you truly experience a supernatural strength that takes you through the fire without being burned. Today, may your joy sharpen the countenance of a friend. Strength and joy come from the Lord's place. May you choose to go to Him today so that you overflow with both these gifts. May you sing for joy as you remain in the shadow of the Lord's arms and see Him scare away all that threatens your peace.

Hope in the Lord today and let Him keep your joy tank full. May you know that the Lord puts more joy in your heart than those who find their prosperity elsewhere. You have all you need in Him.

24

Stay Blessed in the Silence

Romans 8:28, 10:17; Proverbs 2:1–5; Psalm 25:4–5

I f you find God to be silent today, may you choose the perspective that God is fighting your battles and something powerful is about to happen. May you have a deep understanding that His silence is not evidence of Him not hearing your prayers or listening to you but rather the opposite—He is working it out for you and can't speak right now. Something good is about to happen.

May you listen to Him with the same passion and desire that you want Him to have when He listens to you. May you trust, believe, hold on to, and follow His words. He has security and blessings waiting for you. Your life depends on you listening to God. May your faith grow as you hear God and wait on Him. God is faithful. He will reveal His work and power in His time.

25

Be Armed with Strength

Psalm 18:32, 37:23, 84:11; Isaiah 25:1; Matthew 6:33;
Luke 10:38–42; Jeremiah 10:23

May God arm you with strength today for all that you have to do. May the path you walk be kept secure by God alone. May you trust God's counsel that you heard long ago because He is faithful and true. May the truth you hold on to give rise to praise and bring to your memory the wonderful things God has done for you.

May you take many moments to build your strength and faith through rest. May you value rest and appreciate the purpose and gift in it. May you look to God to create your schedule. May you complete what God sets out for you to do today and celebrate those victories. There are so many things that are wanted. There are also so many that are needed. May you take both to Jesus. May you let God order your steps today, and as you walk in them, may you receive the blessings He has for you.

26

Go High

Isaiah 55:8–9

May God share His thoughts with you today and cause you to dream, have greater faith, take risks, and believe Him for more. His thoughts are higher. His ways are higher. He is more. He can do more. May you look up, reach up, and take a step up. Dare to go higher to meet with God. Dare to go higher to see God do amazing things. Dare to take the high road of forgiveness. Dare to go higher in a spiritual discipline—pray more, praise more, fast. Exercise your mustard-seed faith.

May you take God at His Word and watch His Word be proven. May His Word come alive in you, for you, and through you. God is His Word. He is alive and well. Get ready to experience what He has promised.

27

Know You Are a Treasured Child

Psalm 17:8, 57:2, 103:17, 136:26; Zephaniah 3:17; 1 John 3:1; Ephesians 2:10

May you hear God whisper His words of affection and love into your ear today. May you know that you are the apple of His eye and that He's looking on you with pride. May you be drawn into His loving embrace and stay there. You are His child. He is honoured to call you daughter. He is honoured to call you son. Let Him hold you, lift you, and carry you.

Your Abba father-daddy will never leave you. He will never leave you alone. He will never leave you struggling. He will never leave you the way you are, as He has so much in store for you. He has big plans for you. You were created for a purpose. He will never leave you without His love. His love for you is everlasting.

28

Know You Are Forever Loved

Romans 8:37–39; Psalm 139; John 3:16; Deuteronomy 7:9;
1 John 4:9–11

May you know that there is nothing you have done, are doing, or ever will do that will separate you from the love of God. His love reaches you wherever you are. When you sit and rise, in the dark or in the light, His love calls you. His love hears you. His love is for you. He made you who you are and loves you that way. You are fearfully and wonderfully made. You are unique and uniquely loved. There is only one you. The one and only God loves the one and only you.

Remember this truth. God so loved you that His Son died for you so that you can live in love. God keeps His covenant of love with you. Grow in His love as you keep His commands, and know that God remains faithful in His love to you for generations to come. God loved you first, loves you still, and will love you last. You are forever loved.

29

Remain in God's Love

John 15:9, 13; 1 John 4:8; Jude 1:21; Ephesians 3:17–19; Isaiah 54:10

There is no greater love for you than the love of God. He has laid down His life for you in great love. May you allow His great love to build your courage and erase fear. You can be bold in His love. His perfect love casts out all your fears. When you're afraid, remember that He loves you. When you have doubt, remember that He loves you. When the enemy comes to lie to you and fill you with guilt, remember that He loves you and you are forgiven. Keep yourself in the love of God.

Remember that the devil is always a liar, and God is always truth. Abide in Him and His love. May you be rooted and grounded in His love and grow to understand the breadth, length, height, and depth of His love for you. May His love fill your every thought and every space in your heart. Things and people will come and go in your life, but God's steadfast love will always be with you.

30

Continue in His Steadfast Love

*Psalm 52:8; 1 Peter 4:8; Mathew 22:37–39; 2 Thessalonians 3:5;
Lamentations 3:22–23; John 13:34–35; 1 Corinthians 13:4–8*

As you continue to trust in the steadfast love of the Lord, may you be like an olive tree that produces continually for the glory of God. May you always know how much you are loved and love yourself that deeply so that you can love others freely. Keep loving others with the love you have received from God. Your love will be a blessing and cover over a multitude of sins. As you love the Lord your God with all your heart, soul, and mind, may you continually be filled with His love to love your neighbour as yourself. God loves to use you to show His love.

May the Lord direct your heart to His love and keep you steadfast in Christ. As you stay in Him, you will bear much fruit. May you experience a new expression of God's love for you today and every day. His steadfast love never ceases and is new every morning. May you find joy in God's love and how His love overflows to others through you. He loves you so much. Love others as He has loved you. Let your love be the testimony that you are a child of God. His love is the greatest and will never end.

31

May His Presence Keep You

Psalm 16:11, 42:1–2, 84:1–2; Colossians 3:16; Romans 15:13;
Isaiah 26:3

May the presence of God change your mood and perspective today when they're not pleasing to Him but detrimental to you. May an attitude of worship create an attitude of expectation and joy. May a whispered or shouted prayer, however you need to deliver it, carry you into a deeper place of intimacy and safety. May one scripture verse of truth transform your mind. May the Word of Christ dwell in you richly and lead you into the perfect will of God for you in this season, moment in time, situation. May the presence of God strengthen you like never before as His joy fills you and keeps you in perfect peace.

32

A Great Work

Genesis 50:20; Romans 8:28; Hebrews 12:2; Philippians 4:19;
Isaiah 64:4

May you look for great blessing in what disappoints you. May you see God at work bringing you a breakthrough from the very thing that tried to break you down. God is always working something better in what didn't work out. Shift your focus to Jesus. Look to Him and not at what is happening around you. Before your answers to prayer come, may you give an answer of praise and peace to your worries. Settle it in your soul that you choose joy, you choose trust, you choose Jesus. May God's provision surprise you and remind you that God goes before you and makes a way. May you believe that God is doing a great work in you, through you, and for you. Trust Him and wait for Him to come through for you. He will. That is truth!

33

Trust His Truth

Romans 8:31; Jeremiah 29:12; Philippians 4:8; Ephesians 3:20–21

May you walk with the certainty that God is for you. May that truth mean more to you than the number of those against you. Only one opinion, one force of power, one presence matters! May you know that God's thoughts toward you mean more than even your own thoughts of yourself. His are the truth. His are always good. His always bring life. May you trust what God can do. He can do anything and everything. Expect. Anticipate. Wait. Rejoice.

34

Go and Grow

Galatians 2:20; Isaiah 30:21; Psalm 143:1, 145:5–7, 9

May you know that you are stronger than you think, because Christ lives in you. You live by faith in the Son of God. May you know that this is a life worth living. May you know that you have all the help you need to live the life you have been called to. From before you were born, God has been faithful. You can truly say that throughout all your life He has been faithful and oh so good!

May you take every opportunity to tell of the goodness of God. May your belief in God, His power, what He's doing in you be evidenced by your quick obedience and steps of faith. May each step teach you how to trust God more as your helper and provider. May each step lead to a lifetime of blessings. May you let go and let God grow you!

35

Expect the Unexpected

Deuteronomy 10:21; Jeremiah 32:27; Philippians 2:13;
2 Corinthians 5:7; Isaiah 64:4; Psalm 9:10, 20:7

May there be a strong sense of expectation and anticipation today that you can't escape. May you look for a miracle because God is always up to something. May you praise Him because He performs awesome wonders! As the sun rises and the moon then takes its position, may you be reminded that each new day, each cycle, is a fresh opportunity for God to display His power. He revives. He reveals. He refreshes. He remains in control. May you trust God, who has already prepared the way over, under, through, or around whatever you are going through. Nothing is too hard for Him!

May you submit and surrender to Him as He prepares you for your breakthrough. May hope rise in your heart. May you move into your future hearing what others cannot hear and seeing what others cannot see. May your ears hear music, victory, and celebration long before you walk into your future. May you see through the eyes of faith the great things God has in store. May you have the courage to dance and shout today because you believe God keeps His promises and you believe His Word.

36

Rise with Hope

Romans 8:1; John 1:1; Philippians 2:8–11

May you rise with hope today. It's a new day. May your heart rejoice again in the truth that Jesus is Lord. May you walk with Him today and allow His presence to strangely warm your heart. May you walk with confidence through any situation in freedom and security, knowing there is no condemnation in Jesus. May you walk according to the Spirit and let Him guide and strengthen you.

Let nothing and no one discourage you. Your Lord has kept His great promise and will keep all others. He is a man of His Word! He has been the Word, created the Word, spoke the Word, kept the Word from the beginning of time. He is Lord, exalted and glorified. May your bowing knee and confessing tongue bring others to the truth you know and already celebrate.

37

A Living Hope

Luke 24:6–7; 1 Peter 1:3; 1 Corinthians 6:14

May the truth of an empty grave and a risen Saviour infuse your day with fresh hope and strength. When others reject you or think that you're not worth their time, may you know that God has chosen you. He rose so that death, shame, condemnation, separation, and so much more would never be able to keep you down. May you look at the empty tomb and know that God keeps His promises.

May you know that you are a living hope! Testify to it! He lives! There is nothing or no one that kept Him down. May you know that in Him, that truth is also your reality. God raises you up from situations that try to pull you down. God will also raise you up to be with Him when it's time. You are promised a future. God fulfills His plans! God completes His work. Walk in victory. It is yours!

38

Understand the Beauty of the Cross

Isaiah 53:5; Luke 23:24; John 19:28–30; Ephesians 3:14–21

May you linger a little longer at the foot of the cross. May what was considered despised be beautiful to you. May your perspective change as you look up and see forgiveness in the Lord's eyes. May you hear Him say "Father, forgive them" and know it included you then and still does. May you hear Him say "It is finished" and rejoice in the victory sealed for you. May you understand the great length to which God went to save you. May you have a deeper knowledge and acceptance of the depth of His love for you. Celebrate that today and every day. Jesus is good.

39

Dwell with Him

Psalm 84, 23:5, 99:5; Proverbs 15:15; John 14:16–17

May it be your heart's desire to be where Jesus is, to witness where He is working and see His power. May you desire to join Him in what He is doing. May you want to dwell in His presence, stay a while, stay close. May you worship up close and personal. You are invited to feast at His table. You are a welcomed guest. He celebrates your arrival. Take it all in. You are surrounded by His glory. May you want to be with Him as much as He desires to be with you.

40

Declare Victory

1 Corinthians 15:57; Romans 8:37; John 1:14, 8:44; Numbers 23:19

May you continue to declare your position of victory in Christ. Satan thought the cross would tear us apart from God, but it only brought us closer. The cross was not a death sentence but a declaration of life and the power of God.

May you know that the enemy is and will always be a liar. May you know that God is and will always be truth! May you know that God is and will always be victory. May you know that God will always have the final word! Look at the victory you've already inherited. Watch and wait for the victory He alone can bring to your life and through your situations. It is promised. It was confirmed. It is sealed. It is yours.

41

Focussed Thoughts

Romans 12:2; Philippians 4:8; Isaiah 26:3; Proverbs 3:5, 16:3

May the thoughts that you pay attention to today become words of life. May your words become powerful actions that change the world. May your actions develop habits that build a character that pleases God. May your character take you to the destiny God has placed in your life. May you slow down when God puts things in your way to slow you down. He sees farther ahead than you can. He keeps you safe and takes you to where you need to go. May you let God keep you whole. May you commit your whole self to Him—body, soul, and mind—and let Him shape you into the best you.

42

See Through His Light

Psalm 121, 18:1, 36:9; Numbers 6:24–26

May you see light through God's light, with God's light, in God's light. The day may be partly sunny or partly cloudy, but may both be a blessing. May you see light bringing clarity where there has been grey for too long. May the shower from the cloud bring relief in places that have been too hot and uncomfortable. May you stay in the presence of the Lord and let Him bless and keep you. As the Lord turns His face toward you, may His peace carry you forward. In the sun or the clouds, may God continue to be your rock and strength in whom you trust.

43

Pray Always

1 Thessalonians 5:17

May prayer be your first, second, third, middle, and last choice today. When you think about how good God has been to you, pray. When you think of a challenge or walk into one, pray. When you hear unexpected news, pray. When you need patience, when you need to hold your tongue, when you need discernment and wisdom, pray. When you're filled with joy, experience breakthrough and victory, pray. When you need peace, pray. When you need healing or are burdened for someone else, pray. When you are tempted, pray. When you need strength and want to raise your faith, pray. When you just want to get closer to God, pray. May you decide to walk in prayer today. Pray in everything and for everything. May you always love prayer. God loves having sweet communion with you … always.

44

Greater Faith Through the Word

1 Peter 2:2–3; Isaiah 40:8; Psalm 119:89–91; 1 John 5:4;
1 Corinthians 15:57

May your faith be greater than feelings. May you desire the pure milk of the Word and grow because you have tasted and know that only God will satisfy. May you want more and more of His truth, knowing that it's only your desire and God's move that increases your faith and power. You don't have room in your life to let fear take up space.

Decide to let faith live and feed it with God's Word. His Word lasts forever and will accomplish what it was sent forth to do! Don't let doubt determine your level of faith but let faith determine your level of doubt. Decrease it by faith! Push through. Get to Jesus. Touch Jesus and see what great power He will unleash in your life.

45

Reflect on the Good

Psalm 31:19, 34:8, 103:2, 107:1; James 1:17; 2 Thessalonians 3:16;
Isaiah 26:3; Philippians 4:7

May you take moments today to reflect on the good in your life. May you start with the goodness of God, because every good and perfect gift comes from Him! May you know that God's peace that passes all understanding will leave you with a calm mind. You will have a strong weapon against every challenge by keeping your mind stayed on Jesus. May you look to Jesus and declare that you trust Him, even when you don't understand what He's doing. Even when you don't yet see evidence of His power in your present situation, may you hold on to the undeniable evidence of His past displays of glory. He is never changing. He is always powerful. He is always good. May your praise and thanksgiving never cease. May your lips constantly tell of His goodness. Because He never changes, you should never stop declaring and counting your blessings.

46

Continue in Peace

John 16:33; 2 Corinthians 2:13; Isaiah 12:2; Psalm 29:11;
Romans 8:28; Matthew 6:10

May God's peace be with you in the midst of every challenge or storm, decision, and step of faith. You don't have to wait for it. It's yours to experience now. His presence of peace will carry you to your places of promise no matter what obstacles try to delay or derail you. May His peace keep you steadfast and strong and continuing in the direction He has laid out for you.

May you walk with God and notice the ease of your travels. May you stop and rest where and when He directs you, noticing how He refuels and refreshes you. May you run when He requires you to pick up speed, and may you notice the spring in your step and how fast things can move with God.

Stay listening, stay watching, stay following God. Stay purposeful, stay expectant of possibilities, stay praying. God has the first and last say about all that happens in your life. There is nothing you or anyone else can do that will stop Him from working all things together for good. God loves you with great passion. God fights for you with great power. Rejoice in His goodness. Relax in His presence. May His kingdom come and His will be done in your life today as it has been declared and released in heaven.

47

Find Him. Find You.

Jeremiah 33:3; John 6:63, 15:16, 16:13; Psalm 57:2; Romans 11:29

May you be thankful for what God has told you and just as thankful for what you are about to find out. Call to Him and listen well to His answers. The words God speaks to you are life. Search for Him like treasure and He will be found. He wants to be found and to share Himself with you. May you be thankful for who He has called you to be and what He has called you to do. May you anticipate and expect change. May you anticipate and expect God to be who He is—always with you, always for you, no matter what comes, no matter where you are. May you know that God has called you. God has gifted you. God has chosen you. You are His. What He has given to you and placed in you will bear fruit.

48

Thankful

Ephesians 3:18; 1 John 4:19; Hebrews 13:15; John 15:16; Jeremiah 1:5

May you be extra thankful for the love of Jesus today. May you know that before the cross, there was a long obedience, a long road of submission, a great choice of sacrifice. Jesus was deliberate and purposeful. He knew what He was doing. May you know how great His love was and still is.

May you follow the example of Jesus and return to Him your best in obedience. May you willingly submit and experience intimacy and power from the one who matters most. May each sacrifice of praise bring rich blessing. May you choose to love Him with everything that is in you. He first loved you. He first chose you. Accept His choice with great love and gratitude.

49

Know His Great Love

Jeremiah 17:7; Hebrews 13:6; Psalm 118:8; Proverbs 3:26;
1 John 4:9–10, 16

May you walk closely with Jesus today. May you humbly follow Him with confidence. May you trust Him fully and obey Him quickly. May you love Him even more than yesterday and enjoy friendship with Him today.

As you reflect on the love and sacrifice of the cross, may you be overwhelmed with gratitude. May your focus on the cross strengthen your commitment to the one who has always been committed to you. He proved it. He sealed it. He displayed it to the whole world because you are worth it.

50

Moments of Power

Psalm 62:8; John 4:24, 12:13; Galatians 2:20; Philippians 2:12–13

May Selah moments be many for you today. May you breathe in His grace and breathe out His praise. May you have an encounter with God that leaves you full yet wanting for more of His touch. May you allow His touch to refine and restore you to who God made you to be. May you be ready to be used by Him because you have spent time with Him and see Him for who He is and see yourself as He sees you.

He sees you as needing Him. He sees you as redeemed. He sees you as filled with His power. He sees you as loved. May you stand out in the crowd as one who worships Him in Spirit and Truth. May you praise Him because you know and trust Him. Jesus came in the name of the Lord with great blessing so that you can go out in the name of the Lord with great blessing. Pause in that truth. Selah.

51

Let Faith Be Your Bridge

2 Corinthians 5:7; Hebrews 11:1; Jeremiah 33:3; Ephesians 3:12;
Proverbs 15:13; Numbers 6:25

May faith be the bridge you cross to reach your destiny. May faith be the bridge you stand on to achieve unity. May faith be the bridge on which you take a rest and receive love. May you take the walk of faith and walk away from fear and doubt. May you hear His still, small voice—God's gentle whisper—loud and clear. May you be assured of His presence today, and may it bring a smile to your face.

52

Be Confident with God's Help

Joshua 1:9; Hebrews 4:16; 2 Chronicles 16:9; Psalm 40:1–2

May you be brave and courageous today. May you face your challenges with confidence because you know the Lord is with you wherever you go. When you're uncertain about what choices to make, may you remember to approach God's throne of grace with confidence. You are welcomed, accepted, and promised help in your time of need.

May every choice you make today create more room for God to show Himself strong. May your choices make you more into the person God desires you to be. May you trust that God hears your prayers and answers them. May you trust Him to move you from unstable places to solid ground. He will give you a firm place to stand. Your courage, your bravery, your confidence in Him will prove to be the best choice you can make.

53

Desire God More

Psalm 73:25; James 1:22–24; 2 Timothy 1:7

May you desire God more than any other desire in your heart. May no desire compare to knowing, seeing, hearing, or walking with God. May you never forget who you are in Christ and whose you are. May you hear the Word of God say "This is who I made you to be and what I have called you to do." Then … do it! May you remember that you've been given power, love, and a sound mind. God has gifted you. May you take His gifts and be all you have been created to be by first being God's child who delights in being in God's presence.

54

Don't Worry about a Thing

Isaiah 43:19; 1 John 4:18; Psalm 119:165

May you let go of your worries. May you hear the message that every little thing is going to be all right. May you sing a new song today. May a new thing spring forth for you today, and may you see and take the road God shows you. May God's perfect love dispel all fear. May you love God's Word and walk in the peace it gives. Let nothing offend you. You are promised great peace. Take it. Keep it. Live it today.

55

See, Hear, Speak

Jeremiah 1:12; Psalm 138:8; 1 Thessalonians 5:24

May your eyes see through clear lenses of faith today. May your ears hear a word of confirmation straight from the throne of God. May you speak truth with a conviction that God looks over His own Word to make it happen. May trust be your choice and fulfillment be your experience. The one who calls you to believe, to wait, to act, to be is faithful. He will do what He says, as He can only be who He has always been.

56

Expect God to Do the Unexpected

Ephesians 3:20; Jeremiah 29:13; Psalm 27:4, 139:7; 2 Thessalonians 3:16

May God do the unexpected for you today because you expected Him to. May you be pleased with His answer of Himself when you don't receive an answer to your whys. Continue to search for Him with all your heart. May God grant you spiritual insight and open your eyes to His power and purpose.

May you go where you need to go, even if you don't want to, because God has asked you to. May your choice of obedience and act of faith lead you to a place without borders. There is so much waiting just for you as you walk with God. May His presence alone bring you peace to accept what you can't see or understand while you wait, believing His power will be unveiled.

57

May God's Word Be Active

Hebrews 4:12

May familiar scriptures and messages from God carry new meaning and impact in your life today. May you come alive with new perspective in life because the Word has come alive. May the Word bring needed change and transformation. May it bring needed hope and healing. May it bring strength and power as you make it your strongest weapon against the enemy. May God's Word be powerfully active today in your heart and circumstances.

58

May God's Love Reach You

1 Timothy 1:14; Psalm 57:10, 63:3

May the great love of God for the world be real to you as the one who's in His laser vision. May you repeat this truth over and over again: "I am loved. Jesus loves me." May His love lift you out of the depths. May His love lift you higher and higher. May His love lift you into His arms. May His love lift you to safety, freedom, strength, and healing. May His love reveal to you His overflowing grace. May you experience God's far-reaching love today. May you feel it reaching for you in a tangible way. His unfailing love is better than life. Praise Him for His love today.

59

Gather with Him First

Matthew 18:20; Exodus 33:14; Psalm 16:11, 73:28

May you "gather" today with many in prayer, because the Lord promises to be present. May you take many opportunities to gather, because the Lord is there with two or more of you, and you want to meet with Him. May you feel the power of His presence going with you, staying with you, and giving you needed rest. May you experience the fullness of joy because you've been with the Lord. May the pleasure of His presence be too much to measure. May it be good to be near God today. May you have much to share about what God has said to you, shown you, and done for you.

60

A Step of Faith

Proverbs 4:11; Isaiah 42:16; Hebrews 6:2, 11:1; 2 Corinthians 5:7;
1 Corinthians 2:5; Psalm 25:4, 39:7

May you step out in faith today. As you take each step, may you look back and see the evidence that God has done just as He promised. As you move forward, may you see the way being cleared for you, confirming what God has called you to. May your faith take you into your future with a conviction that the best is yet to come.

Today is a new day. May you have fresh perspective. May you have new insights from God's Word. May you experience new and greater intimacy with the Lord. May you keep believing and hold on to hope. Miracles happen daily. You are a walking miracle. Keep walking into many more.

61

Trust God

2 Kings 6:16; Numbers 13–14; Psalm 20:7–8

May God open your eyes to see the heavenly army that is with you. May He shift your focus from your challenges to His greatness. May He remind you that He is not afraid of giants but will destroy them for you. May you see through the eyes of faith what God lifts your eyes to see. May you not rebel against God and live in fear but instead trust God. Trust His power. Trust His plans. Trust His promises. He is always the *one* greater with you than anything or anyone against you. Trust in the name of the Lord your God. He does not, will not, cannot fail.

62

His Confidence—Your Confidence

Proverbs 3:32; Isaiah 42:16; Psalm 27:1; John 1:5, 8:12; Matthew 5:16

May you walk in the confidence of the Lord today. The Lord takes the upright into His confidence. May you know that God has enough confidence for you, and all you have to do is move in His. When the Lord is your confidence, you move in His confidence. Walk closely with Him today. May you trust Him even when you don't have all the answers, because you know that He does.

Remember that your confidence is Jesus. May you walk with the light through the dark places and shine. May you walk in the light and radiate warmth and beauty. May you walk in the light and always find your way. May you be the light and bring glory to God.

63

May Your Position Be Christ

Job 1:20–21; Psalm 61:2

May your heart position be Christ, no matter where you are today. May you fall to your knees yet rise in worship before God in the good and bad situations. May you know that even when you hit rock bottom you can still praise God. Let worship arise and pull you up in strength. May you know that even when you hit rock bottom and feel like you've lost everything, God is still God and is still with you. Talk to Him and let Him talk to you. You haven't lost Him.

May you know that even if you hit rock bottom, God deserves praise. He hasn't changed. God will meet you wherever you are and reveal His glory to you. May you be able to say "The Lord gives and takes away, yet I will praise Him … the Lord's name be praised."

64

Meditate on His Excellence

Philippians 4:8; 1 Chronicles 16:7; Psalm 1:2, 9:10; Joshua 1:10

May you meditate on what is excellent and praiseworthy today. May the name of the Lord lift your thoughts heavenward and fill your spirit with power. May you be reminded all day that the name of the Lord is Strong Tower, Shield, Rock, Emmanuel, Shepherd, Healer, Provider, Peace, Way, Truth, Life … just to name a few. May you seek the Lord and call upon Him morning and night. May you stay rooted. May you stay watered. May you stay connected to the vine—your life source.

65

Stand in Your Armour

Ephesians 6; Psalm 46:7; 1 Samuel 17:45

May you put on your whole armour of God today and be confident that you are appropriately dressed and ready for whatever you have to wrestle against. May you use the strongest weapon you've been given and stand behind the strongest protection. You are not fighting a battle you can win in your own strength. It's not a flesh and blood battle. It's beyond you. The principalities, powers, rulers of darkness, hosts of wickedness can't win against the God of heaven and heaven's armies. He fights with and for you. Demons tremble at His name. May you exercise your spiritual muscles. Let God confuse your enemies as you praise Him. Let God cause them to turn on themselves as you bow in prayer. You are taller on your knees than on your toes. Go against your enemy in the name of the Lord God Almighty. God will knock them down. You are standing victorious.

66

Follow God's Goodness

Psalm 23:6, 31:19, 84:11, 119:68; James 1:17

May you know today that "God is good" isn't just a saying but an experience. May you not just think about God's goodness being for others but for you. May you know that God's goodness is his identity and DNA. You cannot separate God from His goodness. His goodness is abundant and stored up for you. May you hide in it and rest in the safety of it. May you be certain of it following you and allow yourself to stay in it. May you continue to walk in the blessings of God, knowing He will not hold anything back from you as you follow Him.

Let Him teach you His goodness. He is and does good. Trust Him and learn from Him. Every good gift, everything you consider good, everything you don't recognize as good— everything that comes from God to you is a good gift because He is good. Always.

67

Hold on to Him

2 Corinthians 4:8–12; Isaiah 41:13; John 16:33; Exodus 3:14;
Revelation 1:8

May every challenge today strengthen your resolve to hold on to the hand of Jesus. May every unwanted surprise strengthen your decision to let the strong arms of Jesus hold you and carry you. May you let Jesus define you and the outcome of your problems. May your problems not destroy you, your faith, or your peace as you let Jesus destroy what stands in your way—in His way. Today as you wait for your miracle, may you know that you're already walking in one. You are a miracle. Whatever happens today, may you remember that Jesus has already had the final word. May you face everything that is out of your control with the one who is in control. May you hear God say to you today "I am still I AM."

68

Do Not Grow Weary

Galatians 6:9; Matthew 7:12

May you rely on the Lord's strength in all you do today. Do not grow weary in doing good. Put your heart into it and you'll be able to keep going. Let the good in your heart guide you and you will have strength. May you know that at the right time, in the right moment, you will be able to see how the Lord has used you to make a difference. Don't give up. Your effort for the Lord's Kingdom will pay off. As you make choices today, may you be blessed in knowing that you have treated others the way you would want to be treated. May you be able to look back on your day with no regrets but with joy because you have pleased God and nothing has stood in the way of your witness. May you enjoy being a vessel of honour today.

69

Smile

Psalm 139, 18:19, 34:5, 118:24, 147:11; Proverbs 15:13;
Deuteronomy 7:9; Revelation 3:8

May there be many moments today when you catch yourself smiling, and may this cause you to remember the faithfulness of God in your life. May you feel God's pleasure with you, and His smile as His thoughts turn toward you. May you experience tangible expressions of His love for you today that come in the right moment to meet your heart's needs. May you and the Lord have sweet communion today at the most unexpected times, in the most unexpected places, through the most unexpected circumstances.

In moments of "No" may you rise with anticipation and expectation of the Next Opportunity—New Opportunity, New Opening—Next Opening. May you believe and see that God is opening doors for you that no one can shut. Walk in the way and through the way He shows you. Keep looking for God at work. Keep following Him. Smile at each other along the way.

70

Look Up. See with Faith

1 Kings 18:41–45; Hebrews 11:1; Psalm 139:14

May you look up and see the "cloud" today. Like Elijah, may you have a perspective of faith and see the first hint God is showing you that your answer is on the way. May what God shows you be enough evidence for you to get excited. Hold on to it with great belief and great faith. God always completes what He starts. He created the cloud and the rain, and He will decide how He wants it to come down on you. Sprinkling or pouring, it is showers of blessings. He may start small, but every movement from God is a blessing.

You never see the whole picture of what God is doing with just one look. Look again. Then look again. And … look again! Let nothing distract you from praying. Let nothing distract you *in* praying. Keep your head low and focused and rise high in determination and expectation. Expect your soon. Expect your suddenly. Expect God to hear. Expect God to answer. When He does, run forward with strength. Do and be all that God has destined for you. Rise and run praising Him. Marvellous are God's works. May you know that fully!

71

Reasons to Worship

Psalm 34, 145; James 1:12; Joshua 1:9

May you believe with all your heart that in every season God is still God. May you choose joy. May you choose thanksgiving. May you choose gratitude. May you choose worship. May you know that if you woke up this morning, you have a reason to bless the Lord. If you got out of your bed—whether happy or sad, slowly or quickly, with struggle or ease—you have a reason to give God thanks. If you're in a dry place or feeling refreshed, if you're in a trial or in a place of great triumph, if you're uncertain or clear, if you're crawling or walking, may your response be the same—may you rejoice and declare that God is alive and well, present and powerful, on the throne and giving victory.

May you hold on to God. He is holding you. May you stand firm in faith. God is standing with you. He is closer than your next heartbeat. May you know that in all of your life and in every changing season, God is still God. He remains the same, leaving you with the same reason to worship.

72

The Lord Is One

Deuteronomy 6:4–5; Mark 12:32; Zechariah 14:9; 1 Corinthians 8:6;
Matthew 18:9; John 3:16

May you start this new day, this new month, with a love and commitment to the old truth that there is only one true living God! When anything tries to take the rightful place of the Lord in your heart, when other passions and priorities try to take Him off the throne, may you go back to your first love and declare "The Lord our God, the Lord is one." May you make a priority of the God who makes you a priority.

May you be encouraged and strengthened, resting in the truth that the one and only God has a purpose for your existence. He has all power to bring to pass all He plans and intends for you. All things come from God. You exist for Him and through Him. From Him are all things and to Him are all things. He deserves all glory. This one God will leave all others to look for you and bring you home if you are lost. This one God has given His one and only son—for *you*. This one God is the one you need always.

73

Ready, Set, Go

Jeremiah 29:11; Isaiah 55:8–9; Psalm 31:24; Philippians 3:14

May you remember this thought as many other thoughts come to your mind today: God has continued to be who He is—good. May you remember that God's thoughts and purposes toward you are always good, even if it doesn't always feel that way. May you follow what you know and not what you feel. Feelings come and go. May you know that although you don't always receive the answer to your prayer in the way you would like, God is giving you His best answer. If your request won't result in God's best, He'll say no. Only His best will do.

When you're moving into what God wants for you but too quickly, He'll say "slow." Your answer to prayer needs Him to be present. Only the best of Him is the best for you. When you aren't yet formed into what He wants you to be, God will give you opportunities to grow. Only the best you is the best for any moment or situation. God will make the request right, the time right, and, through it all, you right. He will honour His promises to you and say "go." May you hear Him say "Go forward, go upward, go with my blessing—go into all you have desired and all I have destined for you. Press on toward your goal. Go in peace and power."

74

Know Your Position

Psalm 18:1, 2, 17–19, 138:3; Isaiah 30:21; John 10:27; Hebrews 12:1–3

May you know that you were never meant to fight any battle on your own. Although your enemies may be too strong for you, may you always know that they are never too strong for God. May you rise in victory from every trap, test, or trick because you know your position in God and the lies of the enemy. Remember that you have gotten up one more time than you have fallen—keep doing that. Your race isn't finished.

May you pray for what you need with boldness, knowing the power in prayer is in how God answers. May your faith be the bridge from where you are now to the spacious place God is taking you to. May your ears hear what God may whisper louder than what the enemy shouts to distract you. May you stumble across your strength in every struggle as you persevere and let God perfect His work in you. May you throw off every weight that tries to keep you down. You were not meant to carry a lot of what weighs you down. Let Jesus carry your burden. Release what doesn't serve you or him. You are being cheered on. He believes in you.

75

Pause Often

Acts 17: 28; Psalm 44:8, 60:4, 62:5–6, 66:4, 84:4; 1 Samuel 12:16

May you find power in the pause today. May you stop long enough to realize the gift in each breath. May you pause often enough to renew your strength with each step. May you pause and notice the beauty of God displayed before your eyes in His creation. May you pause to draw near to Him and hear Him speak His love to you. Don't rush by and miss His messages.

May you pause to lift your voice and hands in praise. May you pause to acknowledge God's presence and realize that you want to experience more of Him. May each pause bring your heart reasons to celebrate the victory—big or small—in each moment. May SELAH be more than a word but a rich experience today.

76

Listen Well

James 1:19, 22; Proverbs 1:5; Luke 11:28; Romans 10:17;
Philippians 4:9

May you listen well and listen quickly today. May you listen to receive love and to give love. May you listen to be encouraged and to give encouragement. May you listen to receive healing and to help give healing. May you listen as God brings you enough comfort to give comfort to others. May you listen as God gives direction and then follow, being an example of obedience and faith. May you listen for understanding, wisdom, and discernment. May your faith grow today because you've been intentionally listening to God's Word. May your day be more blessed than you expected because you practised listening. May you listen, learn, and practise. And the God of peace will be with you today.

77

Live for God

Colossians 3:23–24, 4:6; Ephesians 4:24, 29; Proverbs 16:21, 18:21;
Psalm 19:14

May whatever you do today be done for the glory of God. Work as unto Him and do your best for Him. May you remember that He is the one to please and He will reward you. Wherever you go today, may you go in the power of God. May you remember that you carry His name. Arrive at every destination in the name of the Lord and take His blessing with you.

Whatever you say today, may your words be filled with truth. May the words of your mouth and meditation of your heart be acceptable to God. May whatever you say today build up others and be life-giving. May the Spirit of God in you lead you to new opportunities and open doors. May you be in just the right place at the right time to receive and be a greater blessing than you imagined. There is strength, there is power, there is hope, there is life in the name of the Lord. Blessed are you as you remain in Him to be all you are called to be.

78

Grow in Love

1 Corinthians 13:1–8, 13

May you grow in your expression of love today. May patience be a virtue that shows fruit for you today. May your gratitude for what God has done in your life remove envy. May genuine humility be displayed. May kindness prove to be a stronger response than rudeness. May your heart be blessed by putting others first. May you practise joy and not sweat the small stuff. May your heart be so focussed on God's love for you that it overflows with love for others. May your capacity to love be a sweet sound in people's ears, a force of strength in their lives, and great gain to you and everyone. May the depth and richness of God's love cause you to experience and live out a love that bears all things, believes all things, hopes all things, endures all things. God's love never fails.

79

Hear Him First

Psalm 5:3, 33:22, 143:8

Today as you begin a new day and wake up to news that is ever changing, may you remember that God's love for you remains. May this morning first bring you news of His unfailing love where you can anchor your soul. When you hear of situations that are life altering, may you remember that Jesus' love and presence is never changing. May you put your trust in what He speaks to you, even as you hear other messages. May you be reminded that He has entered your life for the better, bringing you a permanent peace and joy that nothing or no one can take from you. May you know that God's unfailing love rests with you. This morning may you be drawn into God's arms, and may your starting point be His heart. He hears your voice this morning. May you lay all your requests before Him with expectation and anticipation of His answers to come. He will show you the way to go in every situation.

80

Actively Wait

*Isaiah 40:31; 2 Corinthians 12:9; Exodus 15:2; Lamentations 3:25;
Psalm 27:13–14*

As you wait on God today, wait with expectation. Wait with anticipation. Wait with action. May you know that as you wait for answered prayer, for help, for your eyes to see and experience movement, that God is working. It is not a passive wait. God is renewing your strength. His strength is being made perfect in you. You can look back and see that you have made it forward because of God. May you look up to see that you are higher than you thought. He has caused you to mount on wings like eagles. May you stay where He has carried you. Stay in the peace He offers you. Stay in the joy He fills you with. Stay in intimacy with Him. It is your high place above what tries to cloud your vision.

May you keep running and walking. You can do it. You will get there. Don't stop. Take your time. Go faster when you can. Slow down when needed but continue forward. He promises that you won't get weary or faint. Believe Him. Your wait is not in vain. "You" are happening. God is on the move with you and for you. You can be glad. You can sing. He brings you victory. Your wait is a good thing. The Lord is good to those who wait. Be strong and let your heart take courage. That is His word. That is His promise!

81

Know You Are Family

John 1:12;1 John 3:1–2; Psalm 65:8; Ephesians 1:5

May your heart be blessed today to know that you are a child of God. May being adopted into the family of God hold great meaning for you. May you find comfort in knowing that God will look for you, chase after you, continue to find ways to show you that His love is permanent. Your father has lavished His love on you. May you know that what you have received in Christ gives you the right to be a child of God. Nothing or no one can take that from you.

May you see and hear God defending, rescuing, and reminding you that He is taking care of you. You are a member of God's family. You are safe, loved, accepted, spoken for, and claimed. God purposed, planned, and chose to adopt you into His family. You are family on purpose, and the head of the family loves you so much.

82

Know God Has a Plan

Isaiah 55:8–9; Hebrews 13:15; Psalm 50:23, 107:21–22; Matthew 5:6

May the truth that God always has a plan and purpose for what He does and allows be of comfort to you, even when you don't understand why. May you always search for meaning and beauty underneath the heap of what has fallen on you. May you find a moment to jump, run, play, and lift your arms in praise, just because you can and because it will ease your load. There is freedom in that. Try it! The Lord receives your sacrifices of praise. Some days are just cold. May you warm up in God's love and stay close to His heart. Some days are just dry. May the wellspring of life bring you refreshment today. May you hunger and thirst for righteousness and experience the filling God promises. He keeps His promises. May your trust grow today and your faith produce fruit.

83

Celebrate

Deuteronomy 10:21; Psalm 45:6–8, 116:15; Revelation 21:4

May you celebrate today because you choose to and it increases your joy. May you celebrate the gift of a new day. May you celebrate because you have seen God do great things and expect more to come. May you celebrate times spent with loved ones. May you have the opportunity to celebrate the family of God growing because you shared the love of God. May good memories bring you comfort as you remember those who moved home to Jesus and celebrate that Jesus keeps His promises and you will be reunited. May you celebrate the big and small victories. May you celebrate that there are no surprises for God. There may be unexpected situations, but God already knows. May you celebrate because God's goodness is abundant. You can shout joyfully because of His great mercy and love. The Lord is righteous in all His ways. Celebrate so your soul knows that God is still in control no matter what!

84

May There Be a Move Today

2 Corinthians 2:6; John 12:32; Isaiah 59:1; Zephaniah 3:17; 2 Peter 3:9

May today be the day of salvation for those for whom you have long been praying. May you continue to lift God up and trust Him to do His job and keep His promise of drawing all unto Himself. He is the God who saves. May you continue to believe that God's arm is long and can reach where you are unable to go. Let your prayer rise, and know that it reaches His ear. He hears and moves. Nowhere is too far for God to go. No one is too far away from God. God is mighty to save. He is everywhere at all times to save any soul, to save us from our enemies, to save us from ourselves, to save us from sadness and despair, to save us from going in the wrong direction, to save us from missing His presence with us.

May you hear Him sing over you. May His voice bring quiet to your spirit. May His rejoicing over you bring peace to your heart and confirm His love for you. May the mighty warrior show you that He is fighting for you—to save you and your household and all those you bring to Him. He is not willing that any should perish. He had the best battle plan and has already won. He is patient and keeps His promise. Trust Him.

85

Trust His Faithfulness

Psalm 33:4, 116:2; 2 Thessalonians 3:3; 2 Timothy 2:13

As you bow for times of prayer today, may you rise with new strength and fresh purpose. May you look up to see God bending to listen to you and show you how involved He is in your life. May you realize that God is all you need and all you need to know. May you trust Him for what He has provided, prevented, and proven to you. God will guard you and establish you. May God's story and the history of His faithfulness pave the future you walk into. God is always faithful. He cannot deny Himself. May you know that no matter what you do, God's faithfulness remains unchanging. May you trust His Word. All His work is done in faithfulness.

86

Love Truly

Luke 10:27; John 3:23–24; James 2:17

May your worship of God today be alive through serving others. May you live out loving God with all your heart, and your neighbour as you would want yourself to be loved. May you love yourself with enough true love that others receive the true love of Jesus. May God use your life to gracefully love today. May love radiate through your smile, be a strong current through helpful hands, be a sweet melody through your words, and be a life-giving flow through your heart. May you live out true worship today and honour God with all that you are. Be blessed today.

87

Be at Ease in Him

Psalm 25:8, 9, 14; 2 Thessalonians 3:3

May the Lord confide in you today and make His covenant known to you. May you not miss any part of God's message to you because you are so close to the heart and voice of God today. May you follow the loving and faithful path He guides you along. In moments when life may be uneasy, may you be at ease because you spent time with Jesus and He has filled you with peace. May you live out and experience the Lord's presence with you wherever you go, giving you rest from all that seems to drain your strength. May you rest from worry, anxiety, fear, doubt, anger, and strife. May you stay in close communion with the Lord, who is faithful to establish you and guard you against all evil. May today be a day of active listening to the right voice—His. May you be honoured and treasure what He tells you.

88

Know Who Is in Control

*Habakkuk 1:1–5; Matthew 10:29–31; Colossians 1:16–17;
Isaiah 45:7–9; Psalm115:3*

May you be reminded many times today that God is sovereign and still in control. As the problems of this world mount up, may the things of this world grow strangely dim in the light of His glory and grace. May you grow in deep understanding that God is not silent, distant, or indifferent but is patient, compassionate, and still upright and just. He will right the wrongs. He will give His answer to corruption. May you trust God when things seem chaotic—He is still in control.

May you know that God knows about everything that concerns you. You are valuable to Him. May you know that God wants the best for you, even when you have to travel the hard way. May you remember that God Himself has travelled the hard road and claimed victory. Your victory is promised. Your victory is sealed. Your victory is in Jesus. God holds all things together in the world and in your life. God does what He pleases. May you look to the heavens and see His glory revealed today.

89

Listen Well

John 6:63, 10:27; Luke 11:28; Isaiah 30:21

May God's voice be the sweetest voice that you hear today. When He calls you, may you attend to Him above all other voices. May you run to Him and take your time in His presence. May you hear His voice giving clear direction. May you hear His loving voice giving correction that is founded on His good plan for your life. May your heart be soft toward God, and your ears open to His voice. May you listen to His voice speaking words of unconditional love. Today, may you know how close God is because you hear Him speak directly to your need. His words are life. He loves you so much.

90

God, Your Portion

Psalm 73:25–26; 1 John 4:4; Philippians 2:13; Ephesians 3:20

May God be the strength of your heart today. May He be more than enough and the portion you treasure. When your heart and flesh appear to fail, may you remember that God is carrying you and giving you all you need to carry on. May you remember that greater is He in you than He in the world. The Lord has never lost a battle, and He never will. He does not fail at being who He is and will not start failing you now. May you experience God's constant love and power for you, in you, and through you. May you believe God in everything and for everything. He can do all things but fail!

91

May Faith Open Your Eyes

Mark 10:46–52; Philippians 1:9–10

May your faith heal you. May you receive sight in the places where you have been blind. May you want to see. When you see what Jesus shows you, may you follow Him with your whole heart. May you see that you are loved and always have been. May the knowledge that Jesus' death was a deliberate choice change the course of your history and cause you to make a deliberate choice to believe and obey Him for eternity.

May your love abound more and more in the knowledge of Him and what He continues to teach you. May you grow in discernment. May your life be lived in excellence and sincerity as you serve the Lord. May blindness be your past and sight be your future as you let amazing grace do its work. You have been set free. Your God has saved you. He has promised good to you. May His hope secure your faith. May faith keep your eyes open to the life and liberty He has for you!

92

Celebrate His Faithfulness

Lamentations 3:22–23; Isaiah 40:31; Hebrews 13:8

Today may you celebrate endings and rejoice in new beginnings. Celebrate because you have made it this far. Celebrate because God has lifted you, carried you, and held you. Celebrate because God hasn't left you. Rejoice because you are moving into a fresh start. You are one step away from where you haven't been before. May the same hope that you carried through the past carry you into the future. Rejoice because there are new mercies, compassions that never fail, and great faithfulness that can be trusted. Rejoice because as you wait on the Lord, you will have renewed strength and mount higher than you ever expected. Rejoice because God will lift you up, carry you over, and hold you close.

May you know that the Lord who makes a way today makes a way tomorrow ... makes a way any day ... makes a way every day. As you turn the page, the God who is the same yesterday, today, and forever remains with you and for you no matter what!

93

Be Who God Created

Ephesians 2:10; Psalm 57:2; Jeremiah 32:19; 1 Peter 1:23;
Matthew 4:4; 2 Corinthians 9:8

Although there are certain things you'll never be, there are many things that you already are and that need celebrating. May you be and become all God has purposed you to be, and know that He loves you. You are exactly who you are meant to be. Believe God's Word and live it. May you know that knowing the Word of God will help you to stand firm in your faith and on the uncertain rocky road of life.

Get to know His Word. Get to know your God more. May you take in new life by breathing in the very breath of God through His Word, the God-breathed Word, and live today. Live to the fullest. You have all you need. You and God are all you need. You are enough. He is more than enough.

94

Unto the Lord

Psalm 37:5, 90:12, 17; Colossians 3:23; Proverbs 16:3, 7, 9;
Hebrews 4:9–11

May you let God establish the work of your hands. May you work as unto the Lord and experience His blessing. May you ask God to teach you to number your days that you may gain a heart of wisdom. May everything you do and are count for His kingdom and glory, even your rest. May the routine of work and rest flow into a natural rhythm. Even the Lord rested. He wants you to follow His example. He knows best. Rest from your toiling. Rest from yourself. Rest in Him and rise up with strength and purpose every time. If you follow God's lead in your doing and being you will do and be all that you were created for. May you commit your ways to the Lord and watch your success unfold before you.

95

The Lord Is Your Gift

Psalm 20:4, 143:8; Proverbs 19:21; Matthew 6:19–21, 7:7–11

As you think ahead and make plans, may you choose to leave the completion of your plans up to the Lord's will. May you not worry but trust your future moments to God. May you truly seek the *presence* of God and not only the *presents* from God. He does give good gifts, but His greatest gift is Himself. Seek first the kingdom of God, and He has every gift to give to you. Seek him in prayer, and through prayer be drawn into the most beautiful, intimate relationship with the God who can touch your heart like no other. God promises good gifts as you pray, and it starts with the answer of Himself. He will speak to you and confirm His promises over and over. May your treasure be Him. Your heavenly treasure cannot and will not be destroyed. Nothing or no one can take away what God has planned for you.

96

Go with Boldness

Isaiah 25:4, 65:24; 2 Timothy 1:7; Psalm 89:8–9, 107:28–31

May you be bold today as you lift your prayers to God. He is more bold in answering. Before you call, He is answering, and while you are speaking, His listening ears have already heard it all! God is not intimidated by your requests. May you go to Him with the power, love, and sound mind He has given you and leave timidity behind. May you know that the very oceans that may be rising, the thunder that might roar, the wind that may blow—all are created by the creator and subject to His voice. You can be calm because He calms the storm with His voice. As He speaks to calm your storm, may His voice calm your heart. May you know that your God is strong and faithful and that you are as safe as you could ever be in His care.

97

Nothing Overwhelms God

Matthew 19:26; Proverbs 16:8; 2 Corinthians 5:7, 12:9

May all that overwhelms you be put into the hand of God, for whom nothing is ever impossible. As you trust Him to make all things possible, which without His power wouldn't happen, may you be freed up to express praise, after praise, after praise. May you remember that God keeps His Word. His very nature and essence are love, faithfulness, integrity, purity, righteousness. He does not lie. He will not fail you. Failure is not an option!

May opportunities pursue you as you live for Him. May your gifts make room for you, and may God open doors you never imagined opening. Look up and walk into your God-given destiny. You walk by faith not by sight. In your greatest weakness, may you see God's greatest expression of strength and power. May you be overwhelmed in the presence of God by His love and power today. Stay awed by Him. May His power be perfected in you, for you, and through you today.

98

You Are Already Winning

Deuteronomy 31:6, 8; Matthew 5:16; 2 Corinthians 4:6;
Isaiah 54:17; Romans 8:31–39

May you know that God was already present in your today before you arrived. He is already in your tomorrow. He is already taking care of the pain in your yesterday. There is no need to worry about what has happened or what will happen. God is already working on everything in your life.

May you rise today just like the sun, with beauty and power, radiating light to the world around you. May you break the power of darkness and fear as you let the light of Jesus shine through you. You belong to Him. Nothing can come against Him and succeed. Therefore, nothing prospers that comes against you. The enemy starts a loser and ends a loser. You start winning and end as more than a conqueror! Let His peace that flows like a river and His love that moves like an ocean wash over you today and clear your vision to see His power at work.

99

Find Him Faithful

Jeremiah 29:13; Proverbs 16:9; John 8:31–32

As you look for the Lord today, may you know that He will be found. As your heart seeks after Him, He promises Himself to you. May the plans of your heart today be exactly what He has planned. That way, you will be walking with Him and in the direction He has for you.

Abide in His Word today that you may walk in truth and enjoy your journey. The truth sets you free—free to sing, free to dance and skip, free to walk without weight, free to see and hear the beauty around you while not missing anything! May you find the Lord answering your prayers today and doing things you expected, things you took for granted, things you hopefully anticipated, things you patiently waited for, and things that totally surprise you. You will find Him faithful! May you have a blessed day today as you journey with Jesus.

100

Declare Your Victory

Exodus 15:1–2; Psalm 16:8,2, 18:2, 150:6; 2 Corinthians 4:18

May praise and worship fill your heart and flow from your lips, declaring the greatness of God. May you declare your victory because He has and because He is. May you stand firm today. Stand firm in God and where God has placed you, with faith that cannot be moved. May you know that because your gaze is fixed on Jesus, nothing can shake you. Your praise tells the enemy that his intentions toward you have and will continue to fail. Praise with confidence because Jesus is your rock, and the enemy's plans will not rock you. May your praise raise you to the perspective God wants you to see from. May joy help you to look at difficult situations through the right lenses. God is in control. He has you stationed right where you need to be for His glory. Stand your ground today. The Lord is standing with you and for you.

101

Stay Open

Psalm 23, 34:17–18; Nehemiah 8:10

May your arms and heart, your eyes and ears, be kept wide open to receive the blessings of God. May there only be room for the good things God wants to share with you. May His gifts push out, knock out, and clear out all that doesn't belong but has tried to take up residence. May you evict unbelief, fear, doubt, bitterness and grudges, lies and deceit, anger or despair. In the challenges of life, may you let God pour His love and power into the places that hurt, and may He soothe your soul.

May you follow God as He leads you into green pastures and beside still waters. May you let the joy of the Lord be your strength. May you let the one who loves you unconditionally bind up your wounds with His gentleness and grace. May you let Him speak in His tender voice the message of His closeness, strength, and truth—louder and clearer than any other voice. May you allow yourself to fall into His open arms and hold you close to His heart as He keeps His loving eyes on you and His ears attentive to your prayers. May you hear God say "I am here. I am here. I am not leaving. I am here."

102

Remember the Truth

1 Corinthians 3:11; Psalm 91:4, 119:105, Psalm 147:3; Revelation 21:4; Matthew 11:28; 2 Corinthians 12:8–10; Nehemiah 8:10; Hebrews 13:8

Today in the moments when it feels like your world is crumbling under you, remember this truth: Jesus is your firm foundation, and you stand secure. In moments when your vision is clouded by pain and uncertainty, remember this truth: the Word is a lamp unto your feet and a light unto your path. When it feels like your only companions are tears, remember this truth: your God is close to the broken-hearted and binds their wounds. He will wipe every tear from your eyes. Today when you feel too weak to take another step forward, remember this truth: God invites you to come and rest in Him. His strength is made perfect in your weakness. The joy of the Lord is your strength. When your world instantly changes, remember this truth: Jesus is the same yesterday, today, and forever. He will never leave you. Remember the truth. You are His. You are loved. Forever.

103

Dig Deep

Luke 6:48; Psalm 103:1–5, 130:1–8

May you dig as deep as necessary to find the source of living water and the bread of life so that you can drink and eat without limit. Dig deep into His Word. Dig deep in prayer. Dig deep and have your feet planted where you stand strong and will not be moved. Dig deep in praise. Dig your foundation deep on the solid rock.

May you know that as you cry out to the Lord from the depths of your heart, He hears you. He doesn't hold anything against you but has forgiveness and love for you. Hold on to Him. He has redemption in store. Let your innermost being praise the Lord. May you dig deep and forget not His benefits. Remember that you are forgiven, remember your healing, remember your vitality in Him, remember that you are crowned and satisfied in Him. With your roots made strong in Him, you will flourish and nothing will take you down.

104

Believe God

1 Peter 5:10

May you know today that the God of all grace is strengthening you through every challenge and trial. He will perfect what He is doing. May you feel His strength working in you, through you, and for you. May you settle in Him. Settle your heart and mind. Settle your doubts, knowing God has settled everything for you. May you walk in His grace today. He has called you to eternal glory. God said it. Believe it. That settles it.

105

Victory in the Truth

Psalm 139:13–14; Romans 8:1, 38–39; 2 Corinthians 1:20,
1 Corinthians 15:57

May you believe that you are who God says you are. The enemy is a liar every second, minute, and hour of every day! Look to the truth! God's Word is true every second, minute, and hour of every day. May you see God standing for you. He stands in power and strength. He stands in belief. He stands in confidence in who He made you to be. He stands in healing. He stands in protection. He stands in life and love. Giants fall when He stands. He is undefeated. With Him, because of Him, for His glory, you are standing in victory.

106

Desires Aligned

Psalm 37:4–5; Jeremiah 24:7

May your heart's desires be the Lord's desires. As you delight in Him, may He give you the desires of your heart. May the Lord move wonderfully in your heart. May the Lord move powerfully in your circumstances. May He change your heart and your circumstances. With Him there is infinite power, endless possibility, and boundless opportunity for miracles in you, through you, and around you. Expect great things from a great God.

107

Abide in Him

John 15:5; Psalm 16:8

May you abide in God today. Take your time and stay with God. Abide so that you bear fruit today and throughout the whole year. In both prosperity and pain, may you abide so that you will be able to learn to praise God and to trust Him through every season. Today has the potential to present both possibilities and challenges. May your eyes be kept on the Lord so that you will not be shaken. The safest place in every circumstance is in the Lord.

108

Decide with God

Luke 10:42; Proverbs 16:9; Isaiah 30:21, 48:17

May you be able to wisely discern all the tasks God is calling you to do today. Many things and people will call for your attention, but let God direct your steps. May you find pleasure and success in following His ways. Sit at His feet and listen to His voice as many times as you need to. All time is in His hands, and with Him it is never wasted. The Lord establishes your way when He delights in the way you take. Start with Him. Stay with Him. End with Him.

109

He Is Ahead of You

John 14:23; Deuteronomy 28:1; Romans 15:13; Isaiah 52:12;
Psalm 139:5

May you choose to take one step of obedience at a time in the right direction. No matter what's happening around you, may you allow God to fill you with His peace and joy. May His love continue to fill you with hope as you listen to His voice lead you into your future. May you see that He is already ahead of you, laying the steps in front of you that you must take. He is ahead of you covering you with His protection, healing, provision, and strength—His answer to all your needs. As you walk into the unknown, walk with the one who is known and knows you. Trust Him.

110

Appreciate the Extras

John 10:10; Luke 6:38; James 1:17

May all your extras today be seen through spiritual eyes. May extra sleep, or the extra time it took to get somewhere or to do something, be a gift to you. God was giving you rest. God was giving you time. God knows exactly what you need before a word is even on your tongue. The answer is on its way while you are speaking. May you notice all your gifts in whatever form they take. The gifts started the moment you opened your eyes. Receive. There are lots coming today. Receive and be glad.

111

Joy That Passes All

Romans 12:12; James 1:2; Philippians 4:4, 6; Psalm 33:21

May you live your joy that encourages others to live theirs. May your choice of joy ignite a strength that is powerful and lives long. May you know that your peace and joy do not need understanding, only acceptance. God has given you a gift beyond your understanding. Let Him keep giving. Honour Him by continuing to receive. May you fully celebrate God's goodness today.

112

God Is Close

Psalm 34:18, 139:7–10, 145:18; Luke 10:38–42

May you know that God is as close as the whisper of His name. Whisper lots. May your prayers pull you right up into God's lap. Get comfortable. Get cozy. He loves to hold you. Let His message warm your heart. Let His voice soothe your soul. Make room for Him today. He has made a lot of room for you. Receive the joy He brings to you in great measure. His love is overflowing. Let it reach you. Let His touch make the biggest difference in your life today.

113

See God Move

Revelation 3:7–8; Philippians 2:13; 1 Peter 2:9; Acts 20:32;
Ephesians 1:18

May you see God move you from the place people feel you should remain and where they feel you deserve to be, to the place *He* has always intended for you. May you remain in Him and be carried to places you never thought possible. May he make *you* something great, where others said you were nothing. May you know that there's no least or "less than" in His kingdom. You have great value. May you put on your coat of royalty even as you worship the King of Kings for who He is and the inheritance He has given you. You are His.

114

Shine

Matthew 5:15–16; John 8:12; 2 Corinthians 4:6

May God shine His light through you in a way that brightens the day for someone else. May your light so shine that God is glorified and the family of God grows. May you closely follow the light of the world and let Him lead you out of any dark places. He shines, and His light can never be dimmed. Let Him shine through you. May you never be afraid of His brilliant reflection through you.

115

Jesus, Your All in All

Psalm 18:2, 46:10, 61:2

May Jesus be your certainty when the road ahead looks grey and uncertain. When the ground under your feet feels like a slippery slope, may Jesus be your firm foundation. When the answers to your prayers are uncomfortable, may Jesus be your comfort. May Jesus be all He is and you be aware of it all. May He do all you need Him to do while you just be. Be still. He is still God. Always.

116

Know He Is Moving

John 3:8, 5:17; Isaiah 55:10; Psalm 40:5

Just as the wind blows gently or with great force, may you be reminded today that God is always moving in power, even when you can't see Him. May you feel refreshed by His Spirit and witness things move and shift places as His breath passes. Just as the rain falls and makes a difference deep into the soil, may the watering the Lord provides in your life reach your deepest roots and quench thirsts you didn't even recognize you had. Just as the rays from the sun stretch across the earth making a visible difference from morning to evening, may the beauty and warmth of God's light create a breathtaking picture in your life all day long as you reflect on His goodness. Enjoy God today. He is at work in marvellous ways.

117

Know He Considers You

Psalm 8:3–4; Luke 2:10–11

May you consider the stars, sun, and moon—the work of God's fingers—and be reminded that this great, miracle-creating God is mindful of you. He cares. You are of great importance to Him. May you fix your gaze on the one who is worthy of your fixed attention. May you recognize when God stops you to visit with you and enjoy Him today. May you accept His gift of great joy. You don't have to look for it. You don't have to manufacture it. It's not counterfeit. He brings it to you—real, authentic, and in abundance. Let His great joy control your response to every situation. His joy is contagious. You need it. The world needs it too.

118

Know to Count Your Blessings

Luke 1:28; Psalm 8:5, 37:4–5, 90:17; Proverbs 8:35; Romans 8:28

Today may you take stock of all the gifts God has blessed you with. It's good to count our blessings. May your eyes be opened to the abundance you are walking in, and may joy be revived. May you have many moments today in which God speaks His favour over you, just like He did to Mary. May you be reminded like Elizabeth that God remembers you. As you count and take stock, may you be encouraged to take your need to Jesus, knowing that only He can give the best answer and provision. He always has and always will. May today be a day you celebrate answers seen and unseen, because once God is working, it gets done. You are in the best hands.

119

Know to Ponder Many Things

Matthew 1:20–21; 1 Thessalonians 5:16–18

As you ponder many things today, may the Lord visit you in a personal, tangible way and bring you much needed clarity. May you obey and follow His instruction. He is trustworthy. May you give Him thanks for who He is and continue to rejoice in Him. You always have a reason for thanksgiving because He is always present. You always have a reason to rejoice because He is always in power. Live in the will of God and keep your attitude and spirit praying, praising, and filled with gratitude. God is always at work, even if you don't understand what He's doing. He has the answer. He has given the answer. His name is Jesus. He will save us! He has saved us. Be glad in the past, present, and future work of our Lord and Saviour!

120

Know God Is with You

Isaiah 41:10; Joshua 1:9; Deuteronomy 31:8

May "God with you" take on new meaning for you today. May you understand that He is not close, not on His way—but here! He is with you in your rising, your sitting, your eating, your sleeping, your waiting, your hoping, your crying, your laughing, your doing, and your being. He is with you now. He is with you later. He is with you. You are not alone. Praise Him for His ever-abiding presence.

May you step past where you want to be and into where you need to be. Step into worship. Step into a place of thanksgiving and rejoicing. This is God's will for you. Step into your blessing of peace that passes understanding. Step into His arms of love.

121

Know Possibilities with God

Genesis18:14

May you know that whatever is impossible for you is not impossible for God! Your God can do anything and everything. Nothing is too hard for God. No thing will surprise God. No thing will stump God. No thing is a match for God's power, so give Him everything. Give Him all that is too much for you. Give Him what is making your possible impossible. Give Him your limits and stand amazed as He makes limitless possibilities come alive in your life. God will show His appointed time. God will keep His Word. "Is anything too hard for the Lord?"

122

Room with Jesus

Isaiah 26:3, 46:4; 1 Peter 5:7; John 14:27; 2 Thessalonians 3:16

In this time where too many places are full, may you know that there will always be room for you in the arms of Jesus. There is room for you to sit in His lap and be kept in His embrace. In the busy times, may you know that Jesus is never too busy to see and hear you. You don't have to wait in line; you don't have to wait for permission to be given access; you don't have to wait for His attention. He came for you. In the chaos, the uncertain, the hurt, the uncomfortable, the tired, the weariness, He comes in peace. He comes with peace. He is your peace. Your peace is not lost and doesn't need to be found. Your peace is freely given and only needs to be received. May you take a hold of what has been freely given. Only this peace will last.

123

Hear His Whisper

Psalm 32:7, 34:10, 84:11, 91:11, 104:28; Mark 4:22

May you enter this day hearing the whisper of God, reminding you that no matter what is happening around you, you are blessed and highly favoured. May you see something happen today that triggers your mind, heart, eyes, ears—your whole being—to remember that He came to earth for you and has promised to never leave you.

May you slow down and see where God's light is shining and follow closely to where it leads. Let Him lead you to the secret place where you can worship and receive the joy and peace that has been brought to you. The gifts have been given and are waiting for you. These gifts keep on giving in abundance and without measure. These gifts are what you need. Receive and receive some more.

124

Kingdom Come

Matthew 6:10, 19–21, 33; Psalm 65:8. 113:3

May you put Jesus first in all your life and not only in certain areas of your life. May you experience true peace in challenges that may not leave, because the presence of God is with you. May you believe that God's plan for your life is stronger than any momentary setback. There is no delay or circumstance in any day that can prevent God from moving you into your future. May you make the turn with God at end of the road you thought stopped and ended. May you notice each sunrise and sunset and take the opportunity to praise the Lord. May the Lord continue to confirm His creativity, power, and presence in your life. May today be life-changing for you and God's kingdom. May the dawn and sunset hear you join in the shout of joy!

125

Acknowledge Him

Proverbs 3:1–6; Jeremiah 10:23; Isaiah 58:11; Psalm 84:11, 90:17

May you trust the Lord with all your heart today. May you acknowledge Him in the maps your mind and thoughts create. May you acknowledge Him in your emotional ups and downs and wherever your feelings take you. May you acknowledge Him in your speech, song, prayers, physical activities, and spiritual encounters. In all your ways may you acknowledge that you need the Lord, you want the Lord, you are nothing without the Lord, you can only do everything with the Lord, and that He alone is Lord.

As you acknowledge Him, may your eyes be opened to more of His goodness and presence, more evidence that His path is the way to take. May you know that this "little" choice, this "little" shift in perspective, is big in God's eyes. When you offer God your little, the favour of God on you does great things! God knows the when, why, where, what, who, and how for every aspect of your life. May you show up before God, releasing Him to be God and allowing Him to do His best in your life.

126

See What Rises

Psalm 19:1, 27:4; Isaiah 40:26; 2 Corinthians 5:7; Deuteronomy 5:33

May you begin to see the sun rise in dark places, making way for blue skies. May you see that not only light but an array of colour comes when God shines. May you see the beauty of colour that His rays spread and believe that something beautiful, something good is being made out of your life. May you keep going to your God-given destination with God. He is the one who knows the way. He is the only one to follow. May you keep walking and let God keep walking ahead of you. May you let Him keep working while you take one step at a time. While you move, don't miss the displays of His beauty and glory. Stay close to God. Stay focused on God. He has much to reveal to you.

127

Let Him Lighten the Load

Psalm 94:19

May you lighten your burden by letting Jesus do the heavy lifting of the heavy loads you carry. Don't take your time getting to Him and releasing what you should never have held on to. Run to Him and let go. When the cares of your heart are many, may His consolation cheer your soul. Free your arms so that you can receive God's strong and loving embrace. He will pass on His strength, peace, joy, and love. You don't have to wait; they are yours now. They are ready for you to choose to accept them. With empty arms you can raise them in praise. With empty hands you can clap for joy as loudly as you wish. You can place your hand safely in the palm of Jesus. May you keep in step with God's steps and walk closely with Him.

128

When Jesus Calls, Go

Matthew 11:28; Zephaniah 3:17

When you hear Jesus call, may you willingly go. When you hear His voice say "Come to me," may you quickly leave what you're doing and confidently accept His invitation. May you leave your labour, your burden, your worry, your doubt, your hurt and pain, and your fear—leave all that weighs you down.

Don't leave it behind, as you might want to return and pick it up. Leave it in the arms and care of Jesus. Leave it with Jesus in exchange for rest. Receive His rest that turns to strength, confidence, comfort, peace, and freedom. Receive His rest and dance with joy today. Let nothing hold you back. He wants you free and dancing. He rejoices over you with singing. Listen to His song and move to His heartbeat.

129

Know That God is All

John 3:30, 6:63, 10:27–28; Exodus 33:14

When you're at a loss for words, may the Word of God speak to you and through you. May you sit still and allow God's words to comfort your soul, to bring refreshment, to bring much needed healing, to leave you with lasting joy and peace. When life takes you by surprise—good or bad— let the certainty of God's love carry you further. May you focus on who you know and who knows you.

God is trustworthy and faithful. His motives are always pure. May your best surprise today be the closeness of God's presence and the power of His love at work in your life. Whatever you need, whatever you want, God is. No matter what happens today, God is and always will be God.

130

Listen and Follow

John 5:17, 16:33; Psalm 121:4; 1 John 4:4

May your lack of perfection today not be an excuse for a lack of obedience. Even if you're not certain of the way, the how, or why God is leading, when you hear His voice may you be certain of His best for you. May you not only hear what God says but listen intently and follow Him.

He has only spoken truth to you. He has told you all you need to know to have peace. In Him is where you'll find true and lasting peace. As you go through life's challenges, may you remember the honesty of your Saviour. He told you that in this world you would have trouble, but victory is in Him. May you remember that He is with you and won't leave you. He fights for you, has a plan, sees farther ahead than you do, never slumbers or sleeps, and is greater in you than he who is in the world. God is always at work.

131

Keep Moving

*James 1:2–4; Galatians 6:9; Exodus 18:23; 1 Chronicles 16:11;
Romans 12:12*

May God ease your anxieties and frustrations today, clearing the rubble that has fallen onto your pathway. May you be persistent and consistent and not give up. Keep moving forward. You will reach your destination and complete what you started if you don't give up. You will produce fruit. May you trust God to direct you and give you all you need to endure. Seek Him and His strength continually. Seek His presence and you will have His power to overcome. Keep rejoicing. It fuels your hope. Be patient, knowing that this too shall pass and God is always working! Stay praying. God hears and has the power and love to work on your behalf.

132

Expect More

2 Samuel 7:22; 1 Corinthians 2:9; Ephesians 3:20

May all that you have seen with your eyes and heard with your ears confirm the power and greatness of God. May your faith cause you to expect even more of God's power to be displayed in your life. May you believe that there is always more to come, because in spite of what you have seen or heard, there is always more! Your eye has not seen and your ear has not heard what God has in store for you. You are finite and limited, but He is infinite. He can't be put in a box. He knows you love Him, and He loves you even more. He is full of surprises for you and always steps ahead of you with good things planned. Be excited. He does beyond what fills your thoughts and imagination. He does great thing for real! Always. His power is at work within you. He is unstoppable.

133

Know You Are Always Blessed

Psalm 1:1–3; Deuteronomy 28:1–3; Genesis 12:1–3; 1 John 4:4

May you remember today that you are blessed. May you remember that you are blessed to be a blessing. May God's light shine through you to light another's way so that they can give glory to God. May God's abundance be more than enough for others to have enough to receive and share. May His strength that is made perfect in your weakness be exactly what is needed to build you up and help you pick someone up along the way. May you trust God to fill you up when you feel that you're not enough or feel depleted. He will then use you because He specializes in that. Let God be God for you, in you, and through you today. Let nothing hold you or Him back!

134

Know He Carries You

Psalm 118:5–6; Isaiah 40:11, 41:13

May you see the spacious place the Lord is setting you in. He is on your side. Nothing and no one can stop you from reaching your God-given destination. God is taking you there. May you feel the strength and power in His arms as He carries you and lifts you from one place to another. He carries you close to His heart. May you understand the depth of His love as you hear His heartbeat. May you decide to stay in His arms and trust His plan. He will always hold your hand and be with you. May your courage rise as you keep your hand in His.

135

May God Appear

Genesis 32:36, 35:1, 3; 1 Corinthians 10:13

May you have a Bethel moment today as God reveals Himself to you in a new way. May you know that even if you struggle with God, you can hold on and ask Him to bless you. Hold on and don't let go! Pray! Praise! Pray again. Wait in the place where God meets you. May He appear to you again and again and bring you blessings that confirm He has always been with you. God is faithful.

Whatever temptation you go through, may you know that God makes a way out for you and gives you what you need to bear it with success! May your battle plan, your work plan, your family plan, your dream plan, your life plan and strategy start and end with prayer. May you know that once your victory is achieved in prayer, all that you need will fall into place.

136

Wisdom Is Jesus

James 1:5; Proverbs 2:6

May you know that God is always ready and willing to lead and guide you. When you're not sure when to take a step, ask Jesus. When you're uncertain which direction to go, ask Jesus. When your words fail you, ask Jesus. When saying nothing is best for everyone, ask Jesus. When you don't know who, start with Jesus. When you lack wisdom, ask God and it will be given to you in liberal amounts. God will not hold back the abundance of wisdom He wants to share. He wants you to succeed. Ask! There is no shame. There is no rebuke. God is filled with acceptance and love for you. Ask and all the wisdom you need will overflow. Wisdom is Jesus.

137

Anchored Hope

Hebrews 10:23; Psalm 18:1, 33:18, 71:14; Ephesians 1:18

May what you hope for become reality today. May you move from living in awaited promise to fulfilled promise. May your expectation of things to come be filled with more excitement and joyful anticipation. May your hope be anchored in the Saviour, who always keeps His promises. May you put your hope in His Holy Word. May you grow to know Jesus more as you worship Him, and may His truth revealed infuse you with certainty of the hope you hold on to. The Lord is everything you need, and you can trust Him.

138

Lean in to Hear God

Proverbs 3:5–6; 1 Samuel 15:22

May you lean in to hear God speak today. May you listen to Him and follow His direction, even when you don't understand Him. May you acknowledge that He is in control and knows what He's doing, even if you can't figure it out. He is infinite, not you. May you walk in the path He is laying before you. He is directing you. Your steps will become clearer and your paths straighter only as you walk in humble obedience. Obedience is better that sacrifice. He wants you to succeed. Walk in His favour. Trust Him.

139

Peace

Colossians 3:16; 2 Thessalonians 3:16; Psalm 29:11, 62:1

May the Word of Christ dwell in you richly and bring new perspective to your situations. May you know that the peace God gives is like nothing anyone or anything can give. May you know that the peace God gives can never be taken from you. May your soul find rest in God alone. Rest comfortably in Him today. He alone is your rock. Don't let anyone shake you or move you. You have a firm foundation. You are secure.

140

Praise Him with Your Whole Heart

Psalm 9:1–2

May you praise the Lord today for who He is with your whole heart. May you praise Him for what you have, what you are waiting for, and what you may never get. Your Father knows best. His will is good. Praise Him for his marvellous works. Praise Him for His good deeds. Be glad in Him. Be glad in what you find in Him. Rejoice and sing praises to His name! His name is who He is. He is everything to you.

141

Delight in His Word

Psalm 1, 26:12; Romans 10:17; 1 Corinthians 16:13

May you delight in God's Word and meditate on it throughout your day. May you grow in faith as you hear God speak today. May you stand firm in your belief that God has done something, is doing something, and will do something to continue to move you forward in destiny and purpose. May you keep your feet on solid ground. May you praise, praise, praise the Lord today and be filled with joy.

142

Accept His Invitation

Isaiah 1:18

May you accept the Lord's invitation to reason with Him. He wants you to come to Him and accept His love, grace, mercy, and forgiveness. May your spirit be deeply impressed with the truth that the Lord has sacrificed everything and left nothing undone for you. There is nothing you have done or will do that His blood hasn't washed clean. In Him you are all you are meant to be. Accept His invitation. Your time will be well spent.

143

Know He doesn't Change

1 Peter 1:24–25; Hebrews 13:8; Psalm 20:1, 4, 95:6;
1 John 5:14–15; Micah 7:7

In the constant change of moments and days, may you hold tightly to the one who doesn't change. As the grass fades and the flowers wither, may you trust in the one whose Word remains. May Jesus, who has always been who He says He is, be all that you need today. May you rise high because you bowed low in trust, surrender, worship, and reverence. May the Lord who is close and hears your cry answer you today in a tangible way. May today be the day for you! Look to God. Wait on Him.

144

Only Believe

1 Thessalonians 2:13; Hebrews 11:6; Mark 11:24; Ephesians 1:18–19

May you believe God today—not because you feel like it but because you choose to. May you believe God because He is great. May you believe Him because He always keeps His promises. May you trust Him even if it looks like what you're believing for isn't on the horizon. When God speaks, when God moves, when God acts, it only takes a moment for the miracle to be your reality. No one can stop the power of God.

145

Open Your Eyes

Psalm 119:18, 145:18; 2 Chronicles 15:2; Philippians 4:5; Isaiah 55:6

May God open your eyes to see the wondrous things in His world. May your eyes be opened to see the wondrous beauty all around you. May He open your eyes to see the wondrous things He is doing in your life. May the wonder of God be your focus today, and may you be in awe of His power revealed to you. May you know how near God is and lean in. Let Him hold you. Let Him lead you. Let Him surprise you. Let Him show you how much He loves you.

146

Contented Rest

Philippians 4:11–13; 1 Timothy 6:6–12; Job 36:11; Proverbs 19:23; Psalm 43:10

May today be a day of comfortable contentment. May you rejoice in the Lord while you rest in Him. May your spirit be peacefully secure and hopeful. May you walk in true and complete shalom. May it be well with your soul because all is well with you and Jesus. Serve Him and you will spend the rest of your days in contentment. You lack nothing serving the one who is everything.

147

Be Still and Know

Psalm 27:3, 46:10–11; Jeremiah 17:7; Isaiah 32:17; Exodus 14:14

May you be still and know that He is God today. May you know that stillness is a place of power. May you stand in your place of power and let your faith grow. May you wait to see what God is doing and will do with a sense of expectancy. Stillness is a place of confidence. May your courage and boldness rise. Waiting on God is a position of anointing and authority. God's spiritual strategy doesn't make sense to others, but you know whom you serve. You know whom you believe in and are persuaded that He is able to keep that which you have committed to Him. God is in control. He hasn't lost yet and never will.

148

Think on Him

Philippians 4:6–8

As many thoughts come to your mind today, may you think on what is true, noble, right, pure, admirable, and lovely. May you think on the goodness of God in your life. May the clouds of doubt in any moment be broken up by His rays of sun. The Son is shining today. Let Him light your way. Let Him have more space in your heart and mind than any difficult circumstance or disappointment. Let Him fill you with belief as you wait for answered prayer. He hasn't changed. He is still truly present. You wait on the one who is with you. May you keep praying, keep asking, keep thanking. He is listening to your requests. He is still truly faithful.

149

Treasure the Word

Matthew 6:21; Psalm 65:5, 147:11; Hebrews 10:23

May your heart find treasure in God's Word. You will always find value there. He is the Word, was the Word, and will always be the Word. You can trust His Word because He has already kept it. May you see God faithfully answering your prayers and renewing your hope in a future that is secure in Him. God is your hope. He is a miracle-working God. May you feel His delight in you as you put your hope in His unfailing love. May you hold tightly without wavering because God can be trusted to keep His promises.

150

Move with Jesus

Philippians 3:12–14; Psalm 32:8; Proverbs 4:12–14, 25, 16:24

May you move with God and not stay where you want to be or think you should be but where God is asking you to go. May you take in what nourishes you and not what has the potential to hold you back. May you see what God reveals to you without barriers.

Let nothing stand in your way of seeing God, hearing His voice, and following His lead. May today be a day of new beginnings and fresh starts in your journey with Jesus. Press on toward the goal and the prize God has for you!

151

Everlasting Love

John 8:12; Jeremiah 31:3; Psalm 71:5, 116:2, 130:5

May you know what true light is as the Lord illuminates your path. He has promised that you will not walk in darkness as you follow Him. His light will light your way for life. May you answer His call and respond to His wooing as He draws you into the brilliance and beauty of His love. He loves you with an everlasting love! May you allow His loving kindness to bring you closer to His heart. May His love awaken your hope, and may your hope in the Lord birth a stronger trust.

May you wait on the Lord. May you wait on His Word to be fulfilled. May you wait in His strong arms and rest secure. He bends down to listen to you. Keep praying and expecting answers as long as you have breath!

152

Bask in His Love

Romans 15:4; Jeremiah 31:3; Psalm 86:15

May God's Word revive your soul today. May words written long ago be just the right words for you today. May you learn from them and live through them. Jesus is the Word and brings the Word. May the patience and comfort of the scriptures fuel your hope and remind you of the love God has always had for you. He has loved you with an everlasting love. Ever. Lasting. Always been and not going anywhere. Let that truth sink in today.

May you experience God's compassion and grace today in a new way and understand the depth of His patience with you. As He abounds in love and faithfulness, may you bask in the abundance of it all. It's yours to enjoy.

153

Sense Him Fully

Romans 12:12

May you know that the eyes of God see you today, even if you're trying to hide. May the ears of God hear your faintest whisper and your loudest cry. May the arms of God hold you tightly and reach out to catch you when you're falling. May the voice of God speak tenderly into your ears of His love for you. May you hear. May you listen. May God's presence calm your fears and build your courage.

May you rejoice in the hope you have in Him. May you be patient in your trials, knowing God is fully aware of what you're going through. He is making you complete and is about to reveal His glory. May you continue steadfastly in prayer, believing God is answering. You only want His answer. There are many answers out there, but the answer you need is Jesus and from Jesus. Trust Him. Trust His Word. Trust His love.

154

Expectant Hope

Isaiah 9:2, 6–7

Today may you be able to say that all your hope is in the Lord. May you have a certain and confident expectation that God is up to something amazing.

May your dark spaces and places see a great light today. May you experience the reality of your Wonderful Counsellor, Mighty God, Everlasting Father, Prince of Peace's presence like never before.

May you rise with hope today as you bow down and adore your Lord.

Hold On Pain Ends

He Offers Power Everyday

Holy Optimism Provides Expectation

You have a reason to keep the faith. You have a reason to believe. You have a reason to keep hope alive.

155

Know His Presence with You

James 4:7; 1 Corinthians 10:13; Hebrews 10:23; Psalm 27:1, 139:7;
Nahum 1:7

Wherever you are mentally, emotionally, or physically today, may you know that Jesus is with you. May you experience God right in the middle of your messes, working on them and working in you. May you grab hold of every opportunity to see God at work. May you only resist the enemy and not God. May you see God walking toward you on every long road, around every corner, in every dark space, in every low valley, with His arm reaching to pull you up every high, rocky mountain. May your hope be renewed as God shows you clearly that He is near, always. His presence hasn't left you. He sees you. He hears you. You are safe in Him no matter what. He takes care of His own. You belong to Him.

156

Let Love, Love

1 John 4:7–8; 2 Chronicles 6:14; Galatians 2:20

Today may you let love, love you. God is love, and He has so much to give you. May you abide in the love of Jesus. He calls you. He gives you permission. He truly desires that you abide in Him. May you desire what He desires. May you desire to let His love fill your empty spaces and make your filled spaces fulfilled and overflowing.

God keeps His covenant of love. May you know the power of His steadfast love. May you live freely and liberated in the love of the one who loved you without measure and gave His life for you. You are loved. You have been loved. You will be loved. You have been loved forever. It is sealed. You are loved by love.

157

Know How Close He Is

Psalm 139:5, 145:18; Isaiah 52:12; Colossians 2:6–7

May your faith deepen and strengthen today as you reflect on how present God is in your life. May you become more aware of how close He is. He is before you, behind you, with you. In every space and moment, His presence is there. May your heart be filled with gratitude as you walk with Him today. May you know how rooted and built up you are as you remain in Christ. Your faith is established in Him, and nothing can move you. You are strong. Stay strong in Him.

158

Keep the Hope

Mark 9:23–24; Psalm 118:24; 1 John 4:4; 1 Corinthians 2:9;
Romans 8:31–39

Today may hope be stronger than your doubt, even if the clouds haven't been parted. The Son still shines. May you be blessed that you have been given a new day, even if it's not yet what you expected. May you believe change is going to come. God is always doing a new thing. God is always greater than he who is in the world. God is always at work. Things aren't always as they appear. May your spiritual eyes be opened, and may you see that you are surrounded by God and His army. He is for you. May the Lord confuse your enemy, and may you win the battle today. The war has already been won.

159

Receive His Peace

Colossians 3:15; John 14:27; Psalm 107:1

May you let the peace of God rule in your heart today by exercising your free will and making a choice. You are called to peace. May you accept and follow that calling with gratitude and thankfulness. May you be thankful that peace removes doubt, fear, and anxiety. May you be thankful that peace comes with the presence of God. May you be thankful that the peace the Lord gives is in abundance and nothing can take it away. May your faith grow, knowing that you can go through any and every storm with peace because He is our peace and rules the storm. Give thanks to the Lord, for He is good. His mercy endures forever.

160

May You Prosper in the Lord

3 John 1:2; 1 Corinthians 1:4–5; John 4:13–14; Matthew 5:6;
Psalm 34:8

May today be a day of prosperity. May you move forward, grow, and increase in all things. May your soul experience the most growth, and may this bring health to all areas of your life. May you know how rich you are in the grace of God. May you continually allow Christ's grace to enrich all areas of your life through all He speaks and reveals to you. May His truth excite, encourage, and elevate you to another level. May your interaction with the Lord today be more than enough—more than enough to taste and see that He is good, more than enough to quench your thirst and feed you, and more than enough to leave you wanting more of all that God has given you and always wanted you to have.

161

The Lord Bless You and Keep You

Hebrews 13:5; Numbers 6:24–26

May you be content in all things and with all things you have been given. May your most important gift bring you the greatest joy. The Lord is with you. He has promised to never leave you or forsake you. May you conduct yourself in such a way that everyone knows you don't want what they have because you love having Jesus, and He is enough.

May the Lord's blessing and keeping draw you even closer into His embrace. May you know the complete abundance you have in the Lord's blessing. May you know the power you have. May His face shining upon you shed great light on your path and greatly brighten your day. May His grace bring you great calm as you see His gaze looking on you with love. As the Lord turns His face to you, may peace wash over you like a flood. Your Father wants you to have complete Shalom. Receive His complete wholeness and walk in the wellness God has declared over you. He is with you. He is for you. He is always with you.

162

Let God Work in You

John 1:1, 3, 14:13–14, 17:17; Luke 10:17

May God work in your heart and sanctify you with truth through His Word. His Word is truth. His Word is powerful. May God break chains and loose you from whatever holds you back. There is power in the name of Jesus to break every chain. His name is a word. Hold on to His name. Call out to His name. Declare the promises He has spoken to you.

May you be bold today. May you be honest today. May you let your heart speak and ask for what you need in His name. He gives you permission. He gives you the right. In the name of Jesus, you have the victory. No power can stand up to the name of Jesus. He is the beginning Word. He will always be the Word. Let Jesus be and have the final Word in your life and situation today.

163

Guard Your Heart

Luke 12:34; Proverbs 4:23; Psalm 73:26; Matthew 5:8;
Jeremiah 29:13; Philippians 4:7

May your heart be committed wholeheartedly to God, and may you find great treasure. May your heart be guarded by God's Word so that there is a wellspring flowing out of you. May God be the strength of your heart and be your portion—more than enough—forever.

May you see God do amazing things in you and through you as you remain pure in heart. Seek Him continually. Seek Him passionately. Seek Him with all your heart. You will find Him. He promises that. Stay in His peace that guards your heart and mind as you wait on Him. He keeps His promises.

164

May a Fresh Wind Blow

John 3:8; Acts 2:2; Joel 2:28–32

A s the natural winds blow today, may you feel a fresh wind of anointing blow over you and fill you with supernatural power. May there be new hope breathed into every dream and vision. May a refreshing wind pick you up and carry you above every challenge. May you experience newness in many areas as God breathes into the atmosphere of your life today. May you move with a power that fills you and flows out of you. May greatness be accomplished in you and through you today because the breath of God has filled you with life anew.

165

Prayer for Others

Colossians 1:9; John 8:32

As you listen to God's voice today, may you hear clearly from Him who he wants you to pray for. May you pray continually for those you love. Do not cease to pray for them to be filled with the knowledge of His will in all wisdom and spiritual understanding. Your prayers will make a difference in their lives.

May God reveal truth to you in your spirit as you spend time with Him and meditate on His Word. May it set you free to pray in power for yourself and others. May you receive and know the truth that God speaks beyond a shadow of a doubt and be set free to walk in faith—enough faith to carry you and others!

166

May God Thunder

Job 37:5–6; Hebrew 11:1

May God thunder marvellously on your behalf today! May you hear His voice as He clears the way for you! May you hear Him speak to the mountain and the raging seas. May you hear Him speak "Peace, be still" to your soul. May your faith have substance because your hope is built on nothing less than Jesus. May evidence come alive as you continue to trust Jesus. May God continue to do great things in you and for you that you cannot comprehend but that lead you to trust His power more and more.

167

Seek God with Diligence

Hebrews 11:6; Proverbs 16:9; Psalm 16:11, 37:23

May you seek God diligently today, believing that He will reward you because that's what He said and you trust Him to keep His Word. May you extend your faith and please God. May you know that God is good in every way and that in every answer to your prayers His goodness remains. He loves you. He knows best. May you always choose trust, even when you follow God without clear sight. He can see and knows where He is taking you. He is always a good leader. You are never lost following Him.

168

Receive the Gift and Give

James 1:17; 1 Peter 4:10; Romans 11:29; 1 Corinthians 9:15;
Matthew 7:11

May you recognize and open every good and perfect gift that your Father gives you today. Give Him praise with the gift of breath He has given you. Take His joy and move in the gift of strength. Remain in Him and move from moment to moment in abundant peace. May you serve others well with the gifts you have received. The gifts God has given, is giving, and will give to you are irrevocable.

May continual thanksgiving be in your heart and on your lips as you ponder His indescribable gift. Your Father is a great gift-giver. He gives more than you expect and will surprise you when you ask Him. May you follow the example of your Father today and be a generous giver. Your supply will never run dry but come back to you running over!

169

Let His Glory Be Revealed

Habakkuk 2:14

The earth is filled with the knowledge of the glory of God. May you see it revealed in everything you do and everywhere you go. May your eyes be opened to His power at work in nature, in relationships, in your workplace, in your neighbourhood, in your family, and in the places you didn't expect. May you see His glory in the places and circumstances you gave up on. May you see His glory revealed not only to you but in you. He does his greatest work in your heart. Let His glory fill you and overflow through you.

170

Be Forgiving

Ephesians 4:32; Colossians 3:13; Matthew 6:14; Psalm 86:5;
Galatians 5:22–23

May you be kind and tender-hearted today. May every opportunity that presents itself to you to forgive be met with ease and strength. As you remember how much Christ has forgiven you, may you extend the same with much grace. May you bear with each other and choose forgiveness, even if it doesn't feel good, because it's the right thing to do and you treasure your relationship with God and want to keep the channels open. The Lord is forgiving and good and abounding in love to all who call on Him. May His abundance fill you with love, joy, peace, patience, gentleness, kindness, faithfulness, goodness, and self-control. Remaining connected to Him will fill you with all you need to be fruitful today.

171

Recognize Jesus

Hebrews 13:8

Through the many changes that will happen today, may you trust the one who never changes. May you extend your faith to Jesus, who is the same yesterday, today, and forever. May you allow the power that took you through yesterday to be renewed today. May you allow the healing that is needed in your heart to start today, making you stronger for tomorrow. May you look to the future with confidence, knowing that your God has already gone before you. Jesus is the same healer, the same friend who sticks close, the same unconditional love, the same overflowing joy-giver, the same way-maker, the same protector, the same provider, the same hope and peace. May you look into His face and recognize Him today.

172

Walk in His Marvellous Light

1 Peter 2:9

May you walk in the marvellous light that called you out of darkness. May your path be clearer, your steps more confident, and your direction certain. May you know that you are worth so much to your heavenly Father. He chose you to walk in the place of royalty. May you know that you have a purpose to fulfill. You are set apart not to be left alone but to stand out and be marked for great things. Walk in His holiness. Live in His special blessing given just to you. May you gladly proclaim His praises as you live out His calling. He is worthy. He is great. He is doing wonderful things in your life.

173

The Hope You Are Called To

Ephesians 1:18–19

May your eyes be opened today to not only see God at work in your life but to have greater understanding of the hope you are called to. May your inheritance be confirmed because His is. May you know His power that exceeds any greatness. His power is at work in your life. His reign is established. May you know that you are walking in a power that cannot be tamed. May you know the love that comes with this power and embrace it today in a new way.

174

Let the Praise Begin

Proverbs 15:23; Psalm 95:1–2

May you have unspeakable joy today because you have spoken words of life, words of joy, words of strength, and words of peace. Words spoken to uplift in this season. May the answers of your lips throughout this day bring you and those you speak to much needed joy. May your moments be filled with strength because of your joy choices today. May praise, worship, and thanksgiving permeate your atmosphere as God's love permeates your life.

175

Jesus Is in the Fire

Daniel 3:24–26; 2 Corinthians 4:8–9

May you know that there is one who is powerful and stands in the fire with you. Hold tightly to His hand. Stand behind Him and let Him be your shield. You will not be destroyed. Jesus walks with you through every fiery trial. May you know that you have everything you need in Jesus to face every battle. You may be hard pressed on every side, but you will not be crushed! Jesus will carry your load. You may be perplexed, but do not despair. You are not alone. Persecution may come, but you are not abandoned. Jesus hears your every cry! You may be struck down, but you are not destroyed! Jesus will pick you up. He has plans for you. Don't give up in the battle. The Lord is fighting for you. May you know that the truth has already determined your outcome. You have won!

176

God Is Still God

Psalm 31:15, 47:8; Ephesians 1:5

May God remind you that in every season He is still God. May you know that He is never late and you are not forgotten. May you remain steadfast in your faith. The Lion of Judah has the real roar. The real power belongs to Him. He was and always will be in charge. God is on the throne. May you know that as a joint heir your every need is taken care of and your position certain.

177

Let God Restore

Psalm 23:3, 37:4

May the time you spend with God today restore your soul. May the thirst in your soul today lead you to the refreshment God freely gives. May you follow the Lord as He leads you beside still waters. He gives you peace. He brings you calm. Rest in Him. His paths are right. His way is perfect. Delight in Him today. He knows your desires and finds delight in filling them.

178

Wait on God

Psalm 27

May you see the light the Lord puts on your path today and follow it. May you fear no one and nothing because you know that God is with you, and that means you are already safe. May you walk bravely and with great courage because you know your strength comes from God. Who is there to be afraid of? May you see all that oppose you stumble and fall. May your heart be confident no matter what comes at you.

May you be certain of God's presence and power. Even if you're uncertain of His plan, may you be certain of His goodness. May you know that God is there to help you when you call. He will exalt you to where He wants you to be. You will see the beauty of the Lord revealed as you seek Him. May you be confident of seeing His goodness. Wait on the Lord. Be strong. Take heart. Wait for Him.

179

Let the Word Work

Hebrews 4:12; Jeremiah 17:7–8; Psalm 1:1–3

May the Word of God that is living and powerful reach the very depths of your soul today. May your thoughts and perspectives align with God's Word. May they be pleasing to Him. May you be certain of placing your faith in God and standing on His promises. His Word doesn't change. In any and every season it will cause you to prosper. His Word will protect you. His Word will cause you to grow. You are planted, and nothing can move you.

180

Listen to God's Voice

1 Corinthians 16:13; 1 Peter 1:24–25, 5:9

May you decide today to stand fully confident in the truth and power of God's Word. May nothing change your mind. Even as the world changes what it believes and accepts, may you always believe God and accept His ways. Even if it seems as though you're walking alone, may you remember that God is with you, and His angels are in charge over you.

This world will pass away, and you will have to give an account. Your answer to God is the most important answer every day and always. Stay close. Lean in to His voice. The Word of the Lord endures forever. It does not change. Don't give other voices permission to compete with God's voice. He loves you and created you. He wants the best for you. Answer Him with a "Yes, Lord. Yes to your will and your way. Yes, Lord, yes. I will trust you and obey. When your Spirit speaks to me, with my whole heart I'll agree, and my answer will be yes, Lord, yes."

181

Be Generous

Proverbs 11:25

May you be generous today with the love of God. May you be generous with your thanksgiving toward the Lord. May you be generous with words of encouragement, planting seeds and watering them. May you be generous with your joy and anticipation. Expect big things from God. Don't hold back on your faith. You will receive from God what He has promised.

182

Celebrate the Goodness of God

Galatians 5:1; John 8:36; Nehemiah 8:10; Psalm 30:11–12

As you celebrate today, may you celebrate the goodness of God. May you celebrate that your chains are gone and you've been set free. May you celebrate before the Lord with dancing and be holy undignified, giving Him your best praise. May you be strengthened today because you have chosen joy. May your faith be stronger. May your relationships be stronger. May your mind be stronger. May your heart be stronger. The joy of the Lord is your strength. May you be able to testify that God has turned your mourning into dancing and lifted your sorrow. May you not be able to stay silent, because the Lord has done marvellous things for you.

May your life be a bridge for someone to cross into a safe place. May your prayer be the covering and protection that someone needs today. May your hope be the arm that lifts someone up. Whatever you do and wherever you are, may God be the centre and foundation in your life. May people see that God is the difference in you.

183

Begin with Wisdom

Proverbs 9:10; Exodus 3

May your wisdom begin and grow with your fear of the Lord. May you stand in awe of God once again today. As you marvel at who God is, may your spiritual eyes be open to more truth. May your reality make more sense to you as you trust God more. May your understanding deepen because you have spent time in the presence of the Holy One. May you understand His love and power.

May your feet stand on holy ground many times today. May you have a burning bush experience today that opens your eyes to the fact that God will meet you anywhere. Look. See Him. See that He is a consuming fire. He wants your attention. He wants to use you. He has plans for you. You are not dashed aside. May you understand that there is nothing too difficult for God, and no situation can stop Him from working in your life. The I AM is with you. He is all you need.

184

Bear Another's Burden

Galatians 6:2; 1 Peter 4:10–11

May you bear another's burden today, not to make your life heavy but to ease the load on someone else. May you help to carry a load that is too hard for a friend to lift on their own. Take it to Jesus. He will gladly take it.

Lift them in prayer. Lift them with words of encouragement. Lift them with hope. May they see your faith in action so they may see the power of God in real time. May God use you today more than you thought you could be used. May you find new purpose, gifting, and passion in serving others through serving God. You have received the gifts of God. May you use your gifts to serve others. May your life bring glory to God in every way today.

185

Release Your Plans

Proverbs 16:9; Job 42:2; Philippians 1:6; 1 John 2:20

May you know that no matter how you started your day, Jesus started it with you. He is with you always and will never leave you. Release your plans to the Lord, as only His plans succeed.

May His Spirit give you fresh power to finish what you have started while He finishes what He has started. He is a completer of all things. He wants you to be all that you can be today. Live in the moment. Catch your breath. Move in Him and with Him.

186

Seek Him While He May Be Found

Isaiah 55:6; Matthew 6:33; 1 Chronicles 16:11–12; Deuteronomy 4:29; Proverbs 8:17; Jeremiah 29:13

May you seek the Lord today while He may be found. May you find Him in your joy. May you find Him in your sorrow. May you find Him in your busyness. May you find Him in your stillness. May you know that you will find Him, now and later, here, there, and everywhere.

The time is now. The day is today. He may be found in your present moment. Seek the Lord with all your heart. Seek first the kingdom of God, and He will add so much value and purpose to your life.

Every good and perfect gift comes from the Father above. May you treasure your best gift—His gift of life eternal and His ever-abiding presence. He didn't save His best for last! You have been given everything you need, and all other things are *bonus*. The Lord loves you. He loves when you seek Him, and He keeps His promise that what you seek you will find. Walk in the blessing of His promise today with joy and contentment.

187

Wait on the Lord

Psalm 27:14

May you live with courage today. May your courage come from waiting on the Lord. May you be strengthened physically, emotionally, mentally, and spiritually. He is worth the wait. His answer is worth the wait. His revelation of power is worth the wait.

May you expect from God and hold on to anticipation today. He is faithful. He will do what is best. He will give what is best. He is good. Whatever He does is good. You are waiting on the promise keeper. Wait, I say, on the Lord. His timing is perfect because He is perfect in all of His ways.

188

Leave Your Cares with Him

Philippians 4:4–9; Job 11:17–19; Romans 8:24–25; 2 Chronicles 6:14; Psalm 36:7; Ephesians 3:16–20

May a peace that passes all understanding rest within your spirit today because you have left your cares in God's hand and are walking in supernatural power. May you continue to rejoice because the Lord is with you. May you meditate on the truth continually and chase anxiety away. May the voice of hope lead you forward as you rest in the security of God.

May God's love fill your heart because it has filled every other space and is inescapable. God's love is His covenant. It is sure and will never go away. May you take refuge in His love. May you grasp the wealth you have been given in His love. May your roots go deep! His love is power. May you experience God doing more than you ask today with His great power at work in you!

189

Confess Jesus Is Lord

Philippians 2:11; Psalm 19:14, 119: 49–50; Jeremiah 32:17

May you confess with your mouth today that Jesus is Lord. Confess and declare this to those who are lost so they may find the treasure you have found. Declare it to your mountain and stand proud when it crumbles and falls. Speak it loud and clear to your enemy and watch him cower in fear and run in the direction opposite of where God is taking you.

Whisper softly to Jesus what He already knows. Feel His strong arms hold you and see Him take charge and show power at work on your behalf. May the words of your mouth be acceptable to Him. May they be His truth as you remind Him of His words, not because He has forgotten but because you want Him to know that you haven't.

May the meditation of your heart be Christ-focussed. He is your rock and your redeemer. He will show you that nothing is too difficult for Him. May the things of this earth grow strangely dim in the light of His glory and grace!

190

God Is Still Working

John 5:17, 12:24; 1 Corinthians 12:6; Job 34:20

A s you look at the beauty of the fall season today and see the colours break forth, may God speak to you loud and clear about your season in which He is working underground and in the shadows. May you hear Him say that although it looks like nothing is happening, or that all is dying around you, look again. Look and see the truth. May you hear Him say that there is much happening. May you hear Him say that He is creating colour in the dark room. May you know that your roots are being watered and you are still being fed.

Be still. May you rest well as God works. You are still growing and producing. Let the green go ... let go of the old ... let go of the normal. May you embrace the new. May you embrace the regeneration and new birth. Embrace the new signs of life. You are being formed into a better you. You are going to burst forth and rise with strength. You are where God wants you to be at this moment. His divine plan is happening! There is life and light in every place because God is at work.

191

Pray with Your Heart

Matthew 6:6, 8; Hebrews 11:6; Psalm 37:4

Today may you pray with your heart more than with your lips. May you know that your prayers are heard even in the shortest sentence and faintest whisper. Your Father knows what you need even before you ask. May you trust God to meet you in your secret place and to minister to you there. May you trust that you will see with your eyes the answer you have desired and held close to your heart. He will reward you. Keep delighting in Him. Keep seeking Him. Your faith pleases God. You please God.

192

Stand Firm

Matthew 7:24–25

May you be wise and put the instructions of God into practice today as you go about your day. Listen carefully and then follow His leading. He will guide you well. May He be your firm foundation and solid rock. You can trust Him. He does not change. He is faithful and reliable. May you be confident in the Lord today. Know that nothing can come your way and move you if you're established in him. You are safe in His care through any storm. The rains may come and the winds blow strong, but you will not fall because the Lord is your firm place to stand. Stand strong. Stand in prayer. Stand in praise. Stand sure in Him.

193

The Gift of the Holy Spirit

Luke 11:13

May you ask God today to lead you by sweet communion with the Holy Spirit. May you listen intently to His voice and follow Him with confidence. May you value and understand what a priceless gift God wants to give you. Ask! God gives good gifts, and the Holy Spirit is one of His best. You have a friend and partner in power. Receive and be blessed. May you take Him with you today and boldly go where you have never been with expectation and excitement. There is an open space of new opportunity and fresh anointing waiting for you. Don't delay. Ask and receive. Your Father has so much more to give you.

194

Follow His Plans

Proverbs 19:20–21; Jeremiah 29:11

May the plans you have and follow today be the Lord's plans. Only His plans stand. May you follow His counsel and instruction and grow in wisdom. His plans for you are good. He plans to make you prosper and give you hope and a future. Anything He plans for you will give you a desired end. May you look forward to the future no matter what things look like now. God's hope does not disappoint. May you rise with hope today because God awakened you to live in His purpose.

195

Let the Praise Begin

Psalm 95, 150

May today be a day of both praise and thanksgiving. May your heart be filled with gratitude and awe. Praise Him for who He is. Praise Him for His power. Thank Him for His strength. Praise Him for His sovereignty. Thank Him for His ever-abiding presence. Praise Him for His authority. Thank Him for His mercy and grace. Praise Him for the truth of His Word. Thank Him for His faithfulness and for keeping His promises. Today may you have more than you thought you had and more than you expected to give God thanks for. You have so much right now, and by the end of today you will have even more. May you know how generous God is. He has so much in store for you! God is good all the time. All the time God is good because it's His nature! Let everything that has breath praise the Lord!

196

Know Your Heritage

Isaiah 54:17; Psalm 61:5, 119:111

May you know that your rich heritage today affords you the privilege of walking in righteousness. Let those who come against you in any way know that they come already defeated. No weapon against you can stand against the covering and protection of God. No tongue trumps what God has already said to be true about you or your future. May you continue to testify of the Lord's goodness in your life. Make that your heritage. May it be your legacy. May it bring joy to your heart forever.

May you know that God hears you. He knows what has come and is coming your way. He knows how to save you. You have no need to fear anyone or anything else. Because you fear His name, He has given you a heritage of blessing. Child of God, you are taken care of by a good God whose promises never fail.

197

Follow His Steps

Deuteronomy 28:1–2; Jeremiah 29:11; Luke 10:27; 1 Corinthians 15:58

May you walk after the Lord your God today. He knows your dreams and is leading the way for you to accomplish what He has placed in your heart. May you keep His commands and obey only His voice. He knows the best way for you to walk. May you serve God with all your heart. Blessing awaits you. Your good works are not in vain. Trust Him. Hold fast to the Lord and don't let go! He is your safety and strength wherever this journey takes you. Walk proud and with confidence because your partner is Jesus.

198

Lasting Trust

Isaiah 26:4; Philippians 4:6–7; John 14:26–27

May you trust in the Lord today and choose to always place your trust in Him. This is where you will always get your strength. May you hold on to the peace that passes understanding as you exercise your choice of thanksgiving and voice your needs to God. He gives you a peace no one will understand or take away. Victory is yours because victory was, is, and forever will be the Lord's! May you know and experience the Holy Spirit as your helper. Listen to what He tells you and the truth He reminds you of. May you remember who you are and whose you are. You are more than a conqueror because you are a child of the King of Kings.

199

Sing! Sing! Sing!

Psalm 63, 59:16

May you sing today! Make a joyful noise if you have to, but raise a song in praise and thanksgiving. Sing of God's power. Sing of His mercy. Sing of His defence and refuge. Sing loud. Sing clear. Raise your battle song. Raise your victory song. God is with you. God is taking you out of trouble. May you know firsthand the Lord's help and rejoice in the shadow of His wings. May you know His loving kindness that is better than life. May you be fully satisfied, following Him closely.

Look for Him. Long for Him. Thirst for Him. You will see His power and glory. May you know His loving kindness, which is better than life. May your lips praise Him and your hands be lifted up. Lift them high and be open to receive His blessings as you bless Him.

200

Boast in the Lord

1 Corinthians 1:31; Proverbs 27:1; Romans 15:17; Psalm 20:7

May you live today with intention and purpose. May you live today to the fullest and enjoy the gift that it is. It's a present that you can't give back, so live in the fullness of your present moment. May you boast about the goodness of God and His grace. You don't know what the next day will bring, so do not boast about tomorrow. If you must boast, boast in the Lord.

May the things that pertain to God be your reason for any confidence and every joy. Some trust in the might of so many things, but may you trust in the Lord your God alone. Give thanks to the Lord forever.

201

Listen, Seek, Find

Matthew 4:4; John 10:10; 1 Chronicles 16:11; Isaiah 55:6

Today may you listen carefully to the God who speaks life to you. He repeats things He wants you to truly understand and grasp. May you hear His message and not miss anything. He wants you to hear and hold on to every word that proceeds from His mouth so that you can live—not just survive but thrive. Live the life abundant He came to give you.

Seek the Lord while He may be found; call upon Him while He is near. Seek the Lord and His strength; seek His face evermore! He promises that when you seek Him, you will find Him. Be excited about what you'll find. Treasure awaits you!

202

Extend Your Faith

Matthew 17:20; Hebrews 4:16; Luke 11:5–10, 18:1–8; Colossians 4:2;
Psalm 40:1; 1 Chronicles 16:11

May you extend your faith today, even if it's as small as a mustard seed. May you approach God's throne of grace boldly and receive all the help you need. He will extend His mercy. May you be reminded time and time again that your persistence is accepted and rewarded. May you wait patiently before the Lord for your answer and feel His breath wash over you as He inclines His ear to you and listens carefully to your request. May you seek the Lord and His strength. Seek Him continually. He is waiting to bless you with Himself. He is always more than enough. He is always what you need.

203

Grow in Scripture

1 Timothy 3:16–17

May you treasure scripture today, knowing that it is depositing treasure in you. May you seek to know God's truth today with anticipation and expectation that it is sent to make you better and stronger. May you receive God's Word today and allow it to correct, instruct, heal, and transform you.

God is in His Word and is working at completing you. He wants you to be perfect. He wants you equipped and ready for every task and season. May you willingly yield so that you can stay safe and strong and reach your destination. Listen and learn today. It's in your best interest. May God inspire you as He speaks to you. May you profit in more ways than you thought possible.

204

Change My Heart, Oh God

Ezekiel 11:19; Psalm 51:10; Matthew 5:44, 12:34

May the God who changes hearts be invited to change yours today. May you open up those places of your heart that you have kept away from Him. May the places that hurt be healed. May the places that are hard be softened. May the places that are in the dark be exposed to His light. May God's heart be yours. May you love the unlovely, the marginalized, the oppressed. May you pray for those who persecute you. May God reveal to you the places that need to be changed so that you are made more into His likeness.

May the words you speak today show you and others that you are a child of God. Out of the abundance of the heart, the mouth speaks. What is your speech saying about your heart? What is your speech saying about your relationship with God? You are His image-bearer, and the world needs to see who God is ... that He is real and alive and filled with love for everyone. You are His, and He is yours. Walk together in truth today.

205

Set Your Intentions

Isaiah 25:1; Psalm 33:11, 118:24, 150:6; Luke 1:37;
Jeremiah 32:17; Acts 17:28

May the fact that you awoke this morning set your intentions on praise. This is the day that the Lord has made, rejoice and be glad. There is something in this day for you to give and to receive. Be filled with wonder. Look for today's purpose. Live for today's purpose. May your arising today fill you with expectation. Remember that God is a God of miracles. He can do the impossible. Even death couldn't hold Him captive. Even in the grave, Jesus is Lord! He can raise things to life. What do you need? Fresh faith? Bold belief? Dare to dream. Hold on to hope.

Disappointments do come. Life doesn't always go according to our plans, but the plans of the Lord stand firm forever, His purposes from generation to generation. His way does prevail. You cannot stop God. He breaks through and makes you more than a conqueror. Remember the power of the one who woke you up and gives you life. Remember that only He is in charge and in control. Remember that there is nothing too hard for the Lord. Nothing. Remember that in Him you live and breathe and have your being. Raise a praise and live.

206

A Little Longer

Habakkuk 2:3; Matthew 26:38; Luke 24:49; Romans 5:5;
Psalm 63:7, 72:12, 146:5

May today be a day that you linger a little while longer. May you press in and stay in His presence just a little longer. Rest there. Refocus there. Replenish there. Dream there. Catch the vision there. May you sing songs of praise longer and a little louder. Be lifted there. Be strengthened there. Be filled with joy there. Even if it takes a little longer for your answer to come, may you wait in hope a little longer. You will not be disappointed. The answer is on its way. Help is on the way.

May you know that you need God more than anything else and that your need has been met. He is with you. He is for you. You have everything you need. Stay with Him for as long as you need ... always.

207

Agreement with God

Matthew 6:10; Job 22:21–25; James 4:10

Today may you be in agreement with God before you are in agreement with others, including yourself. May you truly seek to please God and start in the place of humility. May God lift you up and place you where He wants you as you position yourself in Him. Today as you pray "thy will be done," may your grasp on control be undone as you let go and let God. May God be lifted up today and all be drawn to Him—to His power, forgiveness, acceptance, peace, truth, and love.

208

Walk in Supernatural Power

1 Corinthians 2:10, 14; Daniel 2:22; Psalm 25:14, 40:5

May you walk in the power and truth of the Spirit today and receive from the Spirit of God all you need to be an overcomer. May you be spiritually discerning, looking for the secrets God only reveals to those who are close to Him. May you have a supernatural encounter, be infused with supernatural strength, and accomplish supernatural things in your natural experience today. May God get all the glory for the wondrous things He has done, is doing, and will do!

209

Stand in Truth

Ephesians 6:11; Philippians 4:1; Exodus 14:14; Matthew 8:27;
Psalm 46:1; Romans 8:28

May your eyes begin to see how big God really is as you magnify Him today. May you see the Lord raise a standard against the enemy. May you rise up and with boldness stand your ground. The Lord will fight for you. He has made you a promise that He will keep. Let nothing move you. Stand in the truth that God reigns over all. The wind and seas obey Him. He will speak into your situation, and everything will be put in its rightful place. May you see how close God is to you, even in trouble, because He is ever present.

May you trust God's plan and believe that He is working His best out and that you are His top priority. He is making you the best you can be as He transforms more than your situation. He is forming you. May you love who He is making you—the likeness of Christ.

210

May Your Love Abound

Philippians 1:9–10; 2 Peter 1:3

May your love abound today as you grow in the knowledge of the one who is love. May you be more discerning because His love guides you, and your heart is made pure through Him.

May His promises be more profound than your problems. May your faith be stronger than your fear. His divine power has been given to you. You have everything you need through knowing Jesus. May you worship Him because He is worthy. Worship Him, because what He has for you is worth the wait. Worship Him because He is with you. Worship Him because that's the strongest warrior cry you can give. Worship Him because His love is abounding in you, and there is nothing else you would rather do.

211

Open My Eyes, Lord

Ephesian 1:18; Psalm 119:18

M ay the eyes of your heart be opened to see God at work. May you see how He loves so you can learn from Him and do like Him. May you see how patient He is with you and with others. May you see the strength He gives and the power He displays. May you see Him answering prayers you have uttered and ones you haven't had a chance to voice yet. May you see Him right where you thought He wasn't and right where you need Him to be. May you see Him clearly, up close and personal.

212

Living Hope

1 Peter 1:3; Psalm 18:28; Isaiah 14:24, 27, 41:13; Job 23:10

May your hope be living today. May you remember that Jesus has already risen from the dead. Your future is sealed. Your victory is already determined. May you be confident that the Lord will light any darkness you walk through. He knows the way you take, and you will come through like gold. God is holding your hand. May you hold tightly to His and be assured that no matter how hard you squeeze, He will never let go! You can't cut off His circulation. In fact, the harder you hold, the better your circulation. His power runs through your veins to give you all you need to keep going. His love never runs out. Nothing will stop God's plans for you. You have a reason to keep hope alive!

213

Know You Are Blessed

Romans 5:3–4; Psalm 139:8–10

May you understand that you have woken up to many blessings. Before you opened your eyes and ears, God was showering you with His good gifts. You are blessed. May this truth transform your thinking, speaking, and doing today. May you live in the power of your blessed state today, knowing that you are alive for a purpose. Continue to persevere, building character and hope.

May you glorify God, knowing that whatever you may be going through, He is in control and with you. Wherever you are and wherever you may go, God is there. You are always in His view. May you keep Him in yours.

214

Pray with Belief

Mark 11:24; Psalm 20, 37:4

When you pray today, may it be more than routine or ritual. May you pray with intention to draw closer to the one who answers you. May you pray with a belief stronger than yesterday's hope. May you ask boldly. May you wait in confidence, knowing that an answer will come. That answer will be His best for you. May the Lord grant the requests of your lips and the desires of your heart. May the Lord make your plans succeed and cause many to see His goodness. May you erupt in praise and thanksgiving at the victory that only God gives you. May today be your day for a miracle.

215

Word of God, Speak

2 Timothy 3:16–17; Matthew 11:15

May scripture that you read and meditate on come to life for you today. May the Word of God speak clearly to your listening ears, speak light in dark places, speak truth where you have believed lies, speak strength and power in weakness, speak hope to disappointment, and speak healing to pain. May God's inspired Word truly inspire, complete, and equip you. May you be intentional about listening to God today. May your intention create blessings that live long and multiply.

216

Be Fertile Soil

Hebrew 10:35–36; Psalm 73:25–28; Mark 4

May you have a deeper and growing understanding today that you are moving toward a great reward as you take each step of faith. May you hold on to your confidence and fuel your persistence and endurance. May you continue to do the will of God, knowing He keeps His promises and will fulfill His Word.

When things get hard and the world turns cold, may you run to Him and not away from Him. Run into His arms and be kept in His warm, soft, gentle embrace. Make God the strength of your heart and your satisfying portion today. May the soil of your heart not be watered with worry, doubt, fear, and unbelief today.

Don't make room for weeds that will choke the life out of you. Refresh your dry places with prayer and praise. Let His water breathe optimism, belief, and faith into you. May you nurture your dreams and future with His truth. May you stay rooted and established Him. Let the storms come. You will not be moved! He is your firm foundation.

217

Share the Gospel

1 Thessalonians 2:7–8; Ephesians 4:29, 6:15, 18; Romans 12:9–13;
1 John 3:18

As you share your life with others today, may you be sharing the gospel of God. May the words you speak bring love and encouragement that build others up. May the places you go be directed by God and bring peace to each space your feet touch. May your hands serve with warmth and compassion. May your ears be a safe place for the secrets of others as you whisper them only to Jesus, the one who can make a difference. May God bless you and make you a blessing today.

218

God's Intervention

Genesis 41–50

May God miraculously infuse your difficult situation with His presence and power. May His plan of intervention be something that only He could dream up and be evidence that there is a God in control and at work. May God make you forget your trouble while at the same time make you fruitful in your suffering. May you watch God turn what was intended for evil into something that blesses you and others abundantly for generations to come. May you continue to praise, trust, and love God wherever you are and wherever your heart rests today. He is with you. He is working on your behalf. He will see you through.

219

Blessed and Blessing

Psalm 119:50, 68, 89–90; Psalm 139, 138:8

May you know that you are blessed to be a blessing and freely share the goodness you have received from a very good God. May you continue to say that "God is good" as loudly and confidently in the bad moments of your life as you do in the good. May you realize that in your painful circumstances, God is trying to heal you and not hurt you. May you remember God's words and be filled with hope. His promises preserve your life.

May you trust God, who is good and does what is good. Let Him teach you. His Word is eternal and stands firm. His faithfulness continues through all generations. May you be cradled in God's love and light today. May it wrap around you like a warm blanket. May it guide you like a well-laid-out map.

May you move your burdens from your hands to His as you lift your arms and open your fingers in praise to Him who is great. He takes your hand in His strong grasp and tenderly wipes your tears. He is aware of your need. He loves you. You are valued. May you measure your worth and wealth by God's love and not your possessions or position.

Before you were born, God knew you and ordained every day. His thoughts toward you are too many to count. Wherever you are, He is there with you. You cannot run or hide. He knows. He sees. He will fulfill His purpose for you. He will not abandon you. His love endures forever.

220

Hear. See. Experience.

Isaiah 30:21, 41:17–20; John 10:14, 27; Psalm 10:14; Luke 1:49

Today may you hear God, see God, and experience God answering your prayers. May you know His voice and may it comfort and soothe your ears. May you clearly see the hand of God move obstacles out of your way as you walk in obedience to Him and He moves you to new places. May you experience His presence and closeness today. May there be transformation and shift that is tangible and lived. May you declare that the mighty one has done great things for you. Holy is His name.

221

Draw Close

Psalm 139

May you be drawn closer to God today as He reminds you that before you were born, He knew you and loved you! May you smile lots today knowing He is pleased with you. May you rest in the love of God, knowing He holds you and never takes His eyes off you. May you rejoice knowing you are one of a kind! You are fearfully and wonderfully made! You are known wherever you are. You are always in His care.

222

Remain Close and Content

James 1:12, 4:8; Hebrews 6:12; 2 Corinthians 4:8, 5:7; Romans 12:12; Isaiah 40:29; 1 Timothy 1:6

May each step forward take you closer to God, where your vision becomes clearer and your faith becomes sight. May you be consistent and persistent in your prayers. May you remain steadfast. Even if your situation isn't comfortable, may you find comfort in contentment because you know God is with you. He will give you strength. May you have much to be thankful for in every little thing. May you hold on to the promises of God and walk into a promising future. May joy take the lead, and may you willingly follow!

Let Him Carry You

Proverbs 3:5; Joshua 1:9; Philippians 4:7; Romans 4:20, 8:27;
Psalm 31:24, 33:18

May you hold space for every emotion you feel today. They are yours, and what belongs to you is valuable. May each feeling be trusted into God's waiting hands. May you be bold and courageous as you make your way to the other side of fear. There is much waiting for you there! May the strength of God be so natural that your mind is filled with supernatural peace. May you find God as He finds you looking for Him and waiting on Him to do the miraculous in your life. May your silence and lack of knowing what to pray give space for God to clearly speak.

Even though you may carry your burden well, may you let God carry your heavy load and give you much-needed rest. May you rest on the promises of God's Word and let His hope revitalize and restore you. His arms can carry your burdens and you!

224

Prosper for God

Psalm 150:6; Isaiah 48:17; 3 John 1:2; 1 Timothy 6:18; Genesis 12:2

May you be excited about how blessed you are today! You woke up and have breath. You are very blessed. May you praise the Lord today with everything in you! May you look forward to all the Lord wants you to gain today! It is the Lord who teaches you to profit and leads you to where He wants you to go. Profit is growth. May you grow in joy, hope, strength, wisdom, peace, and love. May you prosper in your soul and health as you prosper in every other way.

May you realize that every financial and positional blessing is from God alone. May your prosperity be used to bless and grow the kingdom of God. Your prosperity has a purpose. You have a purpose. Plan well. Produce well. Be rich in good deeds today. You are blessed to be a blessing. Live in it. Live it out! Live it!

225

Hold on to the Good Gift

1 Corinthians 15:57; Hebrews 7:27, 10:14; Timothy 1:13–14

Today may you let your Lord's victory and sacrifice define who you are. May you choose to live the victorious life that has been given to you and can never be taken away. May you hold on to the words and messages left to fill you and continually feed you. Hold on to the truth. It is a good thing committed to you. May you hold on to every good thing given to you by trusting the power of the Holy Spirit at work in your life. You have power. Live in it.

226

Receive His Love

Philippians 2:5–8; Luke 19:10; John 15:13;
Romans 5:8, 8:31–32, 38–39

May you be reminded today of how far Jesus will go to reach you. May you reflect on how far He has already travelled to be reunited and reconciled with you. He left heaven to bring to you His love. He travelled to Gethsemane to show you His love. May you believe the truth that He will keep coming after you to save you from the enemy's traps, from your own selfishness, and from deception, fear, unforgiveness, and everything that doesn't serve you.

He came to serve you. He came to seek and save you. May you walk toward Him and meet Him wherever you are and in whatever state your heart is in. He has sacrificed everything for you. There is no need to run from Him. You are already accepted.

May you know that no love is a match to Jesus. God is for you. No enemy is a match for God. May you know that you will never have to fear. He has already decided to graciously give you all things. Greater love has no one than His toward you. You already have it all. You always will.

227

Overcome

Psalm 91; Romans 8:37; Ephesian 3:15–17; James 2:28

May you know that although the troubles come, you overcome! You are more than a conqueror. Your enemies will try to succeed but will fall to your left and right and not come near you! You are under the protection of the Almighty! No weapon formed against you shall prosper. Take your authority and condemn every word that doesn't align with God's word of truth spoken over your life.

May you redeem the time wisely today by making the most of every opportunity. May you be wise and understand the Lord's will. May you choose faith and act on it. Faith without works is dead. Work on your faith. Work on your trust. Work on your belief. Work on showing love. Just do it. Just be it. God is for you. God is with you. You have breath in the moment. You have already begun your day of victory. May you use this gift and live to the fullest—now. Begin with praise and move in power. God is for you. God is with you.

228

Open Access

Psalm 118:24–29; Deuteronomy 28:12

May you already know that today is a good day because it's the day the Lord has made. May you believe for great things today. God is in control. God reigns and the Son shines. May God open windows of blessing for you. May God open doors of opportunity. May He open up the heavens and share His storehouse of bounty with you. May the work you do today be blessed and fruitful. Today you will share your blessings and not be in need. May the Lord give you success as He makes His light shine on you. You are blessed as you carry God's name. Walk in your blessing. Give thanks to the Lord for His enduring goodness.

229

Everything in Him

Psalm 23, 37:4; Jeremiah 31:25; John 14:27

May you know who to look for to find all your heart's desires and more. And may you choose to delight in Him. Delight in His goodness. Delight in His mercy. Delight in His faithfulness. Delight in His power. Delight in His presence. Delight in His love.

Everything you need, you find in Jesus. Everything you're looking for, you find in Jesus. Everything you think you've lost, you find in Jesus. For every question you have, the answer is Jesus. May you know that only God can fully satisfy and replenish you. May you take the gift of peace from Jesus. He doesn't take it away. He gives it freely and wants you to keep it. Receive and rest well in it. You shall not want for anything trusting Him. Be full today.

230

Firm Foundation

Psalm 119:165; 1 John 5:4; 1 Corinthians 16:13–14; Ephesians 6:10

May Jesus be your firm foundation today. May you stand firm in the truth of His Holy Word and let nothing shake you. May your hope be secure in Him. May nothing cause you to stumble as you hold on to the great peace God gives you. He gives it to you because you love Him and His Word.

May you keep watch today, guarding your heart and the truth of God. Look for His Word to come alive in your reality today. May you stand fast in your faith. Faith is the victory that overcomes the world! May you be strong and brave! Whatever comes at you, God can handle! Be strong in the Lord and His mighty power!

May whatever you do today be fed by God's love. Let Him fill your heart with His love and power. Let that love flow through you to others. In Him you are secure. You are everything you need to be. You are and have more than enough to give. May you be sure of whose you are so you can be all that you are called to be today.

231

Experiencing God

Psalm 116:1–2, 5–8

May your love for the Lord grow deeper and stronger today. As you talk with Him, may you know that He hears your voice and accepts your supplication. May you call out to Him as many times as you desire, all day long. May you experience the grace, mercy, and righteousness of God preserving you today. May you find rest in Him as He saves you from sadness and despair, anxiety and worry, hopelessness and fear. May the abundance and generosity of the Lord's presence, strength, comfort, joy, and love fill your heart and experiences today. May your praises and thanksgiving be lifted today and rise high because God has ministered to you in your places of need. He is listening to you. He sees you. He loves you.

232

Prosperity of God

2 Corinthians 8:7, 9, 9:11; Proverbs 10:6, 22; 1 Timothy 6:6;
Deuteronomy 8:18; 3 John 2

May you be rich today in every way. May your life be filled with right choices so you may grow in the rich blessings of the Lord. May you treasure how rich you are in adventure and experience. May you value how rich you are in health and provision. May you desire to become richer in knowledge, wisdom, grace, kindness, and love. May you truly value serving God and be content with the riches He provides. God makes you rich in every way so that you can be generous. May your generosity today cause many to see the goodness of God at work in their lives. May you remember always that it is God who gifts you with every type of riches. His blessing has made you rich because He is a covenant- and promise-keeping God. May you prosper as your soul prospers and declare with confidence that "it is well with my soul."

233

Cry and Laugh with God

Psalm 16:11, 42:1–8, 56:8–9, 147:3; 1 Peter 1:8; Philippians 4:4;
Zephaniah 3:17

May you experience the love of God on your journey through whatever emotions you encounter today. When sadness fills your heart, may the God of all comfort meet you in that place, just as He has promised. He is close to the broken-hearted and binds up their wounds. When the tears flow, may you feel Him wiping them away and collecting them for you. God is with you and always will be!

May you put your hope in God and praise Him when you soul is down. He will help to lift you. When laughter fills you and is released from the depths of your being, may supernatural strength be shared with others. May you hear God joining you in the celebration. He rejoices over you with love. In every moment, God is present. He commands His loving-kindness to minister to you in the daytime and leaves a song with you in the night. Evidence of His love is present 24/7.

234

Let God Carry You

Psalm 55:22; 1 Peter 5:7; Isaiah 46:4, 8–10

Today may you know that you don't have to handle your problems—
you only need to hand them over to God. Cast your cares on Him
and He will sustain you. Give Him your anxiety because He cares for
you. May you feel the touch of God, who knows every hair on your
head, lift you and carry you to a place of rescue and safety. May you
rest confidently in the one who knows your beginning and end as He
fulfills His purpose in your life. No matter what happens today or any
day, God is the only God, and there is no one like Him. He knows what
is to come because He is the beginning and the end. You can rejoice in
that powerful truth. May you enjoy joy today. The Lord gives it to you.
It is your strength.

235

Believe What God Says

John 8:32, 14:6; Isaiah 30:21; Deuteronomy 31:8; 2 Corinthians 12:9;
Joshua 1:9; Exodus 34:6–7; Matthew 11:28; Psalm 43:3, 13, 55:22;
1 Peter 5:7; Numbers 23:19; Nehemiah 8:10

May you believe who God says you are today because you believe who God says He is. May you believe He is the way, the truth, and the life so that you can follow His whisper as He leads you saying, "This is the way; walk in it." May you believe the truth that can set you free. May you believe that God is always with you and will never leave you so that you can do all things with the strength He gives you. May you believe that God's strength is made perfect in your weakness so that you can be bold and courageous.

May you believe that God is merciful and gracious, patient and full of love and forgiveness *for you* so that you will go to Him with all your burdens, just as you are, and know you are accepted. May you trust that God doesn't lie but keeps His promises so that you can keep the faith. May you believe that God is the one who heals so that you can be sustained in places and times of sickness and be restored to health. May you believe that God is the glory and lifter of your head so that the joy of the Lord can be your strength. May you know that God is enough so that you can say enough to the lies because you know the one who always tells the truth. He says that your life has purpose. Live in your purpose on purpose.

236

Accept His Invitation

Matthew 11:28–29

May you go to Jesus at His invitation with your strife and everything heavy that you carry. May you exchange your load for His rest. May you learn from Him what it looks like to walk in peace. May you follow His example and have a heart that is gentle and lowly yet very strong. May every hurt, doubt, question, anxiety, feeling, and thought that doesn't serve you well and mutes God's voice be silenced as you lean in to hear His continual message of support and love. May you hear Him clearly as He softly calls you: "Come to me. Come to me. Come to me." May your soul be at rest in Him.

237

Let Your Groan Speak

Romans 8:26; Nahum 1:7; Psalm 136:1–3

May you know that even a groan is a message shared with God when words fail you. The Holy Spirit helps you in your weakness and makes intercession for you. May you feel His presence and hear His voice when you need it most, and know you are not praying alone! May every breath you breathe be a reminder that you matter and God has a plan for you. Even when life is hard, may you live in the truth that God is good. May you never forget to remember the goodness of God. He is always good because it is His nature. He is good and His love endures forever. Trust in Him and He will take care of you.

238

Let the Lord Fight for You

Exodus 14:13–14; 2 Chronicles 20; Psalm 37:23, 91:11–13; Jude 24–25

May you hold on to your peace today as you let the Lord fight your battles for you. Stand still in Him and see the victory He will bring you. May you continue in praise and feel the power that it brings as you watch God set ambushes against your enemies. Power and might are in the Lord's hand, and no one can stand against Him. May you give thanks to the Lord because He is with you and His love endures forever.

You are surrounded by a great army that protects you. His angels are in charge and will bear you up, even if you trip. May you walk in the authority given to you to trample your enemies. Rejoice, for your steps are ordered of God. May you hold on to the truth that the Lord will keep you from falling because He has all power. He will joyfully present you as faultless. You are victorious in Him.

239

Encourage Yourself in the Lord

1 Samuel 30:6; Psalm 42

May you talk to your soul and encourage yourself in the Lord today. May you ask yourself the right questions and direct yourself to the answer God has already given you time and time again—put your trust in God. May you decide "Yet will I praise Him." May you pause with the purpose of listening and hearing from God because you know He gives the best messages that feed your soul. May you trust God ahead of time for what will only make sense when you look back. From the very depths of your soul, may you cry out for the very depths of the only well that can fully refresh you. May you choose to stay with God. He will never leave you. He never has, and He isn't about to start now.

240

Know God's Heart

Proverbs 9:10; 1 John 4:10

May you grow in wisdom as you respect God's power and stay in awe of who He is. As you grow in knowledge of Him, may you gain understanding and have fresh perspective. May your eyes, ears, and heart be opened to receive the goodness of God, in spite of what circumstances appear to be. God loves you! He loved you first. He loves you still.

May you know that God's plans for you are always grounded in His goodness and love. You may not feel like God is working but may you always know and believe that He is—on your behalf and for your good. His love doesn't change. His promises never fail.

241

Train with God

2 Kings 6:16; Psalm 25:1–5, 144:1–2

May confidence rise in you today as you prepare to face the day and whatever it may bring. May you expect victory because you trained with God before engaging with others. May God open your eyes to the truth that those who are with you are greater in number than the enemy you see in front of you. May your steps and decisions be strongly rooted in prayer. May you turn to God first so that you can face each obstacle with power. May you take refuge in His strong arms and let Him lift you to your many places of triumph. May you keep looking to God with certainty that you will not be put to shame. No one who hopes in God will ever be put to shame. You are more than a conqueror! The Lord will show you His ways and guide you in His truth. May you follow Him boldly and closely. Stay near. Your success is found in Him alone.

242

Be Content in God

*1 Corinthians 10:31; Philippians 4:4, 12; 1 Timothy 6:6; Isaiah 58:11;
Psalm 1:3, 107:9*

In whatever you do today, may you glorify God. He is the reason you are able to eat or drink or do anything and everything. May you do all your living to the glory of God. May you rejoice in the Lord always, not because everything is perfect but because God is good. God is near. May His closeness help you to learn in much or in little to remain content. May you know that following God with a contented heart is great gain for you. You are rich in Him.

May you see clearly how God has kept His promise to always guide you and satisfy you. God's good things keep you well. May you continue to long for Him and hunger for the things of God. He satisfies the longing soul, and the hungry soul He fills with good things. May you be like a tree planted by water, bearing much fruit today because you put your trust in God. He is your satisfaction that does not fail and never leaves you dry.

243

Trust Him

Hebrews 13:8; Psalm 23:2, 46:10, 125:1–2, Colossians 3:15

When life around you keeps changing, may you keep trusting the one who is the same yesterday, today, and forever to take you safely through. May you pray for calm and feel the peace of God rise within you as He leads you beside still waters. May you close your eyes and find yourself hiding in the arms of Jesus. May you trust in God and not be shaken. Be Still. He is God. May you let the peace of God rule your heart; choose peace and be thankful. God wants right in your life in the midst of all the wrong in the world. Trust His plan. Trust His ways. Trust Him.

244

Likeminded

Philippians 2:1–2; Proverbs 3:5–6; John 12:32, 13:34; Ephesians 4:32;
2 Corinthians 9:6–7; Luke 9:23–24; Mark 14:35–36

May you be likeminded with the Spirit of Christ so that you can please your Lord and complete His joy by being in one accord with each other and love others well. May you walk in the paths God directs as you trust Him. Follow Him as He leads you to share about His love and power. Follow Him as He leads you to forgive. Follow Him as He leads you to be generous. Follow Him as He leads you to surrender and let go so that you can receive with open hands all that He deems best for you. May you walk in full obedience today, sacrificing everything for the one who has already sacrificed everything for you.

245

Moments with God

John 15:5–7; Psalm 9:1, 22:3; Philippians 2:13; Proverbs 8:10; Matthew 6:26, 10:31

May there be many moments today when you choose to pause and connect with God. You can do nothing apart from your connection to God. Abide in Him. May there be many moments today that you choose praise and thanksgiving. He dwells in the praises of His people. You will find God there.

May you choose to focus today on what God has the power to do in you and through you instead of what you can't do. May you choose God's instruction and knowledge above the riches this world offers you. May you know that God has already declared you more valuable than all your eyes see. He has chosen you! May you accept that He is proud of His choice. He loves His choice. May you love your choice. May you know that your moments with God are never wasted. They are the richest moments of your day.

246

Guard Your Heart

Proverbs 4:23, 19:9, 21; James 1:17; Psalm 27:1

Today may you guard your heart above everything else that you want to preserve and protect. May today's choice to do that well determine your life's course. May there be a shift that clearly demonstrates the power of God at work in your life. May it be easy for you to trust God and His heart of goodness toward you, even in your moments of uncertainty.

Every good and perfect gift comes from God. May you let go of what you can't control and let the one who is in control keep the control. You have nothing and no one to fear. He does all things well with wisdom and love. May you let the Lord establish your ways. Trust His plans. They are better than anyone and will be all you need.

247

The Knowledge of God

John 8:32; Ephesians 2:8–9; Colossians 3:2, 16; Hebrews 4:12, 11:6; 2 Timothy 3:16–17

May you grow in knowledge of yourself so that you grow in knowledge of God. May you see who you are not just as you see who God is. May your eyes be open to your need of the one who can save you from yourself. May you become more aware of God's abundant grace and your need for it. May God open your eyes to the prison you have put yourself in, and your heart to the way out that He has made for you.

May God organize your thoughts and give you fresh perspective as you look to Him. May you give His Word freedom to release His power to do the best work in you! His Word is active! Walk in faith today and know that you please God. He will honour you. He will honour His Word. He loves you.

248

Hear and Live His Truth

John 10:27; Romans 10:17; Jeremiah 3:33; Hebrews 12:6; Matthew 4:4; Luke 6:45; Ephesians 4:29

May you hear God's voice clearly today and receive the message He speaks to you. May you accept His truth, peace, strength, love, and even discipline. God's heart toward you is good. He is shaping the best you out of your submission and obedience. Hear and live as you nourish yourself with the words that proceed from the mouth of God. May your heart be filled with the abundance of God's love and truth so that your life can be a blessing to many. May your words impart grace to all you speak with today. May your communion with God be rich as you seek to hear and see Him through all you hear, see, and do today.

249

Keep Following

Psalm 16:8; Philippians 4:13; Zechariah 4:6; Ecclesiastes 3:14

May you set the Lord always before you and not be moved from obedience and faith. May you set Him before you to be your guide and your direction. May you follow Him with confidence and certainty, no matter what the path looks like, because you know His voice and trust His wisdom. May you keep moving forward and never give up. You have Christ giving you strength, so you can do it! It's not your might or power but His Spirit giving you everything you need. Nothing stops Him, so nothing can stop you as you remain in Him.

250

Run and Keep the Faith

Hebrews 12:1–3; Isaiah 40:31; 2 Corinthians 5:7; Isaiah 65:24;
Philippians 1:6

May you continue to run and not grow weary, because you are running the race set before you with endurance and you are keeping the faith. You are anointed, and the Spirit of God lives in you. May God's Word light your path so that you know where to walk and when to take your next steps. You will walk and not faint as you walk in the Spirit and away from the worldly desires that may call to you. Keep walking by faith and not by sight.

May you look up and see that the Lord sees you. His eyes are on you. As you open your mouth to share your requests, may you know that the answer is on its way. His ears are open to your prayers. He is El Roi, the God who sees you. He is not going to leave you incomplete. He who began his good work is faithful to finish what He started. Keep going with your eyes fixed on Him and in His strength. You can do it.

251

Live Out Kingdom

Romans 14:4, 8, 17, 15:13; John 10:10

In everything you do and say today, no matter what happens, may you live for the Lord. You are His. May you stand for God, who is the one able to make you stand. Live out the kingdom of God today—righteousness, peace, and joy in the Holy Ghost. May the God of hope fill you with all joy and peace in believing that you may abound in hope by the power of the Holy Spirit. You can have all the power you need today as you give the Holy Spirit permission to move freely on your behalf. Rest and trust the one who wants you to abound and have abundant life.

Choose to think God's way and you will live in victory, no matter the situation. May you focus on what is true, noble, just, pure, lovely, admirable, or praiseworthy. Think about the Lord. Think about His love. Think about His goodness. Think about what His grace has already brought you through. Think on these things and you will walk in peace today.

252

Fight on Your Knees

Psalm 46:1; Isaiah 30:15; 2 Chronicles 20:15; Nehemiah 2:20

Today may you fight your battles on your knees. May you be still and know who is God. Be still not because of fear but in response to faith. Because you know how big your God is, in quietness and confidence you can watch and wait in strength. The battle isn't yours but the Lord's. The God of heaven's armies has sent forth His angels on your behalf. You are surrounded in safety. You are surrounded with power. You can arise. You can build. Build your life. Build your future. Build your faith. The God of heaven will prosper you.

253

Listen to Truth

Psalm 103:13; Micah 7:19; Hebrews 8:12; Isaiah 55:11;
Philippians 3:13

May you watch God do amazing things in your life today, in spite of what you may or may not have done with your life. May you remember that He removes your transgressions and throws your sins into the sea of forgetfulness. He remembers them no more. Don't forget that. Don't let the lies of the enemy and His condemnation hold you back from moving into what God has for you. Don't listen to the father of lies but look to the Son and hear His truth. May God's truth far outweigh the lies.

His truth has already been proven. His truth has already won. His truth has already been spoken and cannot be taken back. Live in freedom today because you can. The Spirit of Truth lives in you. Don't waste another moment in a place and space that was never meant for you. May you forget the things that are behind and reach forward to what is ahead. Press on. The Lord has so much in store for you. You are free. You are loved.

254

Treasure God

Matthew 6:21, 33; Proverbs 10:32; John 10:10; Deuteronomy 14:2; Jeremiah 30:22

May the presence of God be your most treasured blessing today. May you want for more of God. May you believe and choose the God that is enough, always. Where your treasure is, there your heart is also. May you treasure God first and most and trust Him with your heart. Seek first God's kingdom and His righteousness, and the things you are concerned about regarding your life and physical body will be taken care of by God. He knows your every need. May you allow God to take care of you as you seek Him and walk in obedience.

May you do what He has called you to do. May you be who He has called you to be. May you be rich toward God because He has already been rich toward you. His blessing makes you rich. He has given you everything in giving you His Son. He came to give you life in abundance. May you receive in fulness the blessing He came to give. It is yours to take. You are His treasure. He has chosen you. May you be His and He yours, living in sweet communion. Nothing shall separate you from the love of God in Christ Jesus. Hold tightly to that promise. It is yours to keep.

255

Newness

Lamentations 3:23; Psalm 96:1; 2 Corinthians 5:17; Psalm 40:3, 98:1

May you experience God in a fresh way today. May His presence be new. May His touch be new. May the joy and peace you live with today be new. May your engagement with God be like never before. Today is a new day. You have never lived today before. His love and mercy are new today, so arise with new expectation. Arise with new belief. Arise with new faith. Sing to the Lord a new song. You are a new creation in Christ, and all things are becoming new.

Let your praise and worship be new so that many will come to know and love the God you serve. He has done marvellous things and won the victory. Today is a new day. You will not walk this way again. Live like you never have before.

256

Walk in the Spirit

Isaiah 40:31, 46:4, 65:24; Hebrews 12:1; Galatians 5:16; 2 Corinthian 5:7;
2 Timothy 4:7; Psalm 119:105; 1 Peter 3:12; Philippians 1:6

As you wait on the Lord, may your strength be renewed because His grace is sufficient for you and He has promised to carry you. May you mount on wings like eagles, taking over wide territory and soaring high above your difficult situations. May you continue to run and not grow weary, because you are running the race set before you with endurance and are keeping the faith.

You are anointed, and the Spirit of God lives in you. May God's Word light your path so that you know where to walk and when to take your next steps. You will walk and not faint as you walk in the Spirit and away from the worldly desires that may call to you. Keep walking by faith and not by sight.

May you look up and see that the Lord sees you. His eyes are on you. As you open your mouth to share your requests, may you know that the answer is on its way. His ears are open to your prayers. He is El Roi, the God who sees you. He isn't going to leave you incomplete. He who began His good work is faithful to finish what He started. Keep going with your eyes fixed on Him and in His strength. You can do it.

257

Stay Spiritually Minded

Colossians 3:2–3; Romans 8:1, 5–6; Acts 26:15–18;
Deuteronomy 28:1–14

May today bring you fresh perspective and renewed hope. Set your mind on things above and stay hidden in Christ. He is your protection and security. Live according to the Spirit, and you will live in freedom and above condemnation. May you be spiritually minded and live today. Live in peace.

May you rise today and stand tall in spiritual confidence, knowing that God has met with you so that you can testify of Him. May you be convinced that no matter what you've done in the past, the Lord has qualified you for the future. May you allow Him to use your life to bring others to Him. Obey Him and walk in your blessing. You are blessed because He says so. You are blessed because He keeps His word. You are blessed because the Lord opens His good treasure to you. Walk in His ways and you walk in complete blessing.

258

The Power of God

1 John 4:4; 1 Corinthians 2:5; 2 Corinthians 4:7; Luke 22:31–32;
Ecclesiastes 3:11, 14; Exodus 34:10

May faith be the currency that pays for all the dreams you or others feel you can't or shouldn't have. As you move toward completing goals, may you move beyond the obstacles with the great power of the one who lives in you. The faith you hold is not what make sense to man, but it fully comes from the power of God. His power in you is your treasure. Your enemy is trying everything to sift you and make you fail, but Jesus is praying for you.

May what didn't happen yesterday be cut loose so you can live free in the moments of today. May today be a new canvas that the Lord makes into a piece of art. He makes all things beautiful, and whatever He does stands forever. May you see the Lord do awesome things with your life, as He has promised, so that all may see the power of the Lord at work—including you. See and believe. Trust and know. Wait and experience. God is who He says He is and will do what He says He will do.

259

Live in His Divine Power

2 Peter 1:3–4; Isaiah 54:10; Romans 8:25; Hebrews 10:23; Psalm 27:14

May you live boldly today in His divine power that has given you everything you need to live a godly life. Because you know Him, you have been given great and precious promises. You lack nothing in Him. Listen to His voice instead of the noise that shouts for your attention. Listen to His still, small voice that whispers peace to your soul. May you experience the kindness of God and know that nothing can take that away from you. It is yours to keep.

May the peace of God fill your life as God extends His mercy to you. His peace is His covenant to you that no one can remove. May you have the fortitude that is fed by patience to wait for the fulfillment of God's Word and promises in your life. Wait with hope and expectation, believing that God always keeps His promises. Be strong and let your heart courageously hold on to your faith in the one who is faithful. Let your faith and patience stay partners as you partner with God. He knows what He is doing. He knows where He is taking you. Be confident and choose endurance so that you can live in fulfilled promise. You will never get to the other side if you don't keep going. You can't stop now!

260

Live in Power

2 Peter 1:3; Luke 10:39, 12:6–7; Matthew 28:20

May God empower you with a power that doesn't serve you but serves others. His divine power has given you everything you need for life and godliness. He wants to use you. May you hear His heart and be His heart. May you sit at Jesus' feet to listen. May you hear Him tell you how much you are loved. May you hear Him tell you His plans and remind you of His ever-abiding presence. May you hear Him speak your worth and value to you.

He is intimately involved in your life. He knows every hair on your head! Because of whose you are, you can live and serve in confidence. May you live in freedom, not because of what is happening around you but within you. There is power at work within you. There is love at work in you. There is God at work in you. Arise in Him.

261

Be with Your Friend

Proverbs 18:24; John 15:13; James 2:23; Acts 13:22;
Psalm 100:5, 149:4; 1 Thessalonians 5:24

May you be God's friend today. He is truly and loyally yours. He is your friend that sticks closer than a brother. He is that friend that loves at all times. He loves *you*. May you laugh with Him today and cry with Him if you have to. He takes pleasure in you. May you walk and talk with Him today. May you follow after His heart and find intimacy, acceptance, and an overflow of treasures that nothing and no one else can bring. He is faithful and will do for you all He has promised. Just be with Him today. Be and let Him do. The Lord is good, and His faithfulness continues to all generations. Enjoy the gifts He has for you today.

262

Intentions

Joshua 24:15; Psalm 103, 18:30, 20:4, 27:14, 34:1, 37:4, 119:44;
1 Samuel 15:22; Romans 12:2, 14:23; 1 John 4:7

May today be a day of fulfilled intentions. May you be intentional in how you serve God. May you be intentional about waiting on His timing. May you be intentional about choosing obedience. May you be intentional about whose life you touch with the power and presence of God. May you be intentional about creating bridges and not stumbling blocks. May you be intentional about lifting a prayer and a praise. May you intentionally delight in Him, knowing you can trust Him with your heart and He will fulfill your desires. May you be intentional about love. God loves you so much. Make Him your first love. Being filled with love, go out and change the world!

263

Live for Jesus

1 Samuel 2:2; 2 Corinthians 12:9; Romans 12:15; Acts 17:28;
James 2:26; Zechariah 7:9; Matthew 25:40

May you rise up and be the best you can be because the world is waiting for you to show them how big your God is. May you declare with your mouth and live with your life that there is no one like our God. May every step you take and every move you make be a testament of God's sufficient grace. In Him you move and breathe and have your being. You are living with power! Use that power to do good.

May you look around and see how blessed you are and make a difference for those who need you to pass on the blessings. Pray. Pray. Pray. Then make your faith come alive! Rejoice with those who rejoice, and mourn with those who mourn. Show mercy and compassion. Be love in action. Live today ministering to Jesus and He will come alive to you and through you.

264

Let God's Work, Work

Psalm 119:130; Exodus 17:11–12; 1 Corinthians 10;
1 Thessalonians 5:18; 2 Corinthians 1:4; Philippians 2:15–16

May the entrance of God's Word into your life and circumstances today bring light. May He open your eyes and ears to His movement in your life. May you better understand what He is doing and begin to believe again that your life has meaning and purpose. May you have friends like Moses who lift your hands up and carry you through the battle, and may you be that friend to someone in need today.

Keep your hands lifted up to God in praise and openness for Him to fill. He will give you what you need to win. May you accept that you may not always be comfortable but that you will always be comfortable if you let God work through your life. Turn your concerns into prayers and with gratitude keep from grumbling so you do not miss your blessings. It is God's will for you to be thankful because He is with you and is working good for you. Hold firmly to the Word of Life so you can shine. Shine brightly today for His glory.

265

Stay Praying and Believing

Romans 15:13; 1 Samuel 16:7; 2 Corinthians 10:4; 2 Peter 1:3;
1 John 4:4

May your home be filled with prayers and your heart always ready to extend forgiveness and acceptance. May you see what God sees as you look at the hearts of those He allows in your life. May you ask for godly wisdom, as things are not always as they appear. May truth be revealed to you as you fight the very real and painful physical experiences that are before you. Your spiritual weapons are mighty through God. You have the power to take captive all that stands against Christ. Don't give up.

May the God of all hope fill you with joy and peace in believing—believing His promises, believing the best is yet to come, believing that no matter what happens or how He answers your prayers, God loves you unconditionally, believing that everything you need for life and godliness is found in Him. Believe in Him and you will have more hope than you can imagine as the Holy Spirit fills you and encourages you. Greater is He that is in you. You have all you need to face the world.

266

Move Ahead

Mark 10:27; Psalm 18:34, 121:4; Proverbs 20:24

M ay you open your heart to believing in possibilities, because with God all things are possible. May you trust and pray that change will come, even if it doesn't today, because God never slumbers or sleeps and is always at work. May you worship in the wait and have a new song on your lips because God has touched your heart with His ever-abiding presence. May you stand firmly on the promises of God and jump freely to higher places in Him. He makes your feet like deer and causes you to stand on the heights. May you continue to walk in faith because your steps are ordered of the Lord. The spaces and places God has cleared for you are yours. No one and nothing can stop you.

267

Remember His Faithfulness

Hebrews 10:22; James 4:8; Psalm 103:1–5; Lamentations 3:23

May your trust in what God is doing in your life grow even more today as you release your faith. Go to God with a sincere heart and full assurance of faith. May you draw near to Him and find Him drawing near to you, just as He promised. He keeps His promises. May you find hidden treasures and rest in every season in the blessings that are sure to come. Don't forget the blessings. Remind yourself of the faithfulness of God. May your innermost being praise Him for all He has done for you. May you know that you are right where God wants you to be and that you are being prepared for what is yet to come. Today is a new day, and new blessings await you. His steadfast love never ceases.

268

Rest Safely in Him

Revelation 4:11; Zephaniah 3:17; Psalms 119:114

May your heart be filled with God's love and closeness today. May there be a sense of awe and wonder as you breathe the gift of life you've been given. As your eyes take in the beauty of God's creation, and your ears hear the sound of His voice through the songs of the birds, may your spirit be continually lifted to a place of praise. He is worthy of it all. He is worthy to receive glory and honour and power, for by Him all things were created, and by His will they exist.

May you have child-like faith today. Run to God with speed and freedom. Jump into His arms. Stay with Him and dance with Him as He sings over you with His love and shows you His delight. Take time away from the distractions of this world and make Him your hiding place. Put your hope in His Word. The Lord is your mighty warrior. Rest safely in Him today.

269

Security in Jesus

James 1:5; John 15:7; 1 Peter 5:7; 2 Corinthians 12:9; Isaiah 55:11

Today may comparison not be an invited thief into your space to steal your joy. May you allow God to be the one to know the answers, for He knows everything. May you be okay asking Him questions. He shares His wisdom liberally. May you spend more time thinking about what God thinks of you and less of what others think. May your insecurities be put back in their rightful place as you share them with God and He whispers back to you how secure you are abiding in Him.

May each negative thought of pain, fear, or worry that you share with Jesus draw you closer to His heart and make it easier for you to release all your burdens to Him. He cares deeply for you. May you boast gladly of your need for Him and the weaknesses you give to Him so that Christ's power may reside in you. As He whispers back that you are fearfully and wonderfully made, may your dignity and confidence rise within you. May God's message to you be the most important voice you listen to today. He tells you the truth, always. His Word goes forth and does not return void but accomplishes everything in you that is needed. Let Him have the final word.

270

Say Yes

Isaiah 6:8; Luke 1:38; 2 Corinthians 1:20; Revelations 16:7;
Matthew 4:19

May you start your day saying yes to the one who wants to give His best to you. May you say yes to His voice as He calls you to grow in intimacy with Him. He knows you and wants to hear your heart's desire and you to hear His. He wants you to know Him more and more. He wants you to share your hopes and dreams, your passions and fears, your discomfort and disappointments—everything.

He is inviting you to exchange your weakness for His strength. He invites you to exchange your limits for His endless and bountiful supply of all you need. His love has no limits. His power is immeasurable. His provision never runs out. He is unchangeable, unstoppable, unshakeable. Say yes to the places He calls you to. Leave the old behind and move into the new. Go on the adventure with Him to higher heights. Say yes to His voice asking you to follow His way. Say yes to praying, giving, going, believing, forgiving, waiting. Be still and know He is God. Your YES is the answer to your prayers. Yes, Lord, yes to your will and to your way. I'll say yes, Lord, yes. I will trust you and obey. When your Spirit speaks to me with my whole heart, I'll agree, and my answer will be "Yes, Lord, yes."

271

Let Your Light Shine

Matthew 5:16; Psalm 119:105; Hebrews 12:29

May your light so shine before others that your Father is seen and glorified. Shine brightly everywhere and do not hide. In everything you say, may your words light the path of someone walking in darkness. In all that you do, may your actions brighten the space in someone's heart and lighten their load. May your life illuminate the truth and power of God and cause many to be drawn to Him. May your path be lit by God's perfect, proven Word, so that the dark places you may have to travel will be hit with a light that dispels shadows.

May God's presence in your life ignite a passion that fuels a holy, all-consuming fire in every area your life intersects. May your joy in sorrow, your courage through challenge, your praise in pain, your forgiveness in friendship, your patience in problems, your wait in wandering, and your laughter while longing all be a testimony of the intimate relationship you have with God and of His light that fills your life. May it be contagious and flowing so that you can be a reflection of His love everywhere and at all times.

272

Peace Be Still

Matthew 11:28–30; Isaiah 30:15; 1 Peter 5:7; Psalm 62:1–2

May you rest today in the most comfortable, restful place—the arms of Jesus. May you redeem your time well in that place and space. Rest is not being idle. It is not a waste of time. It's one of the most productive things you can do to feed your soul, mind, and body. May your rest in Jesus produce restoration and rejuvenation that gifts you with strength, peace, and gratitude. May your strength surpass your weakness. May your peace allow you to perform in power. May your gratitude be greater than your grumbling.

In your rest, may you receive from Jesus more than you needed, above what you wanted, and more than expected. He is the God of abundance. You may feel your resting is a little thing, but little is much when God is in it. You may feel your rest is significantly nothing compared to what you could be doing. God specializes in making something out of nothing. Cast your cares on Jesus. He cares for you. He is in control. Always. Let the one who controls the wind and the waves, while sleeping in a boat, whisper to you, "Peace, be still" while you put your anxiety, worry, restlessness, fear, doubt, hurt, uncertainty, lack, and need to sleep in His arms. May your soul find rest in God alone.

273

Satisfaction

Matthew 6:11; Psalm 16:8, 37:4, 145:160;
2 Chronicles 20:12; 1 John 5:4; Hebrews 11:6

May you be satisfied today with the daily bread that the Lord provides. May you remember that you prayed for it, and it has been supplied. May the "little things" be recognized as big things because they have come from a *big* God! May your steps that have been ordered actually be taken. As you look to God for answers and direction, may you actually follow where He leads with quick obedience and firm confidence.

May it be said of you that you are a person after God's heart. May you delight in Him and see the desires you have dreamed about become realities. Remain confident that you will see the goodness of the Lord in your life as you move in alignment with Him. May perseverance be your strength. You may not always know what to do, but keep your eyes on the one who always does. May your choice of faith be an easy one in the middle of your struggle. Without faith it is impossible to please God. Faith is the victory that overcomes the world. You are an overcomer one step at a time. May you boldly declare who you know God to be and what you know He can do.

Our God is greater, stronger, higher than any other. Even when we don't feel it or see it, He is working. He never stops. He doesn't slumber or sleep. While He is walking with you, He has already gone before you to make the crooked places straight. May you be diligent in seeking the Lord and following after Him. The desires of the diligent are fully satisfied. Taste and see that the Lord is so good. There is no one who fills your hunger and thirst like Him. He opens His hands and satisfies with good things. May continual thanks be on your lips. Praise the Lord for all the good He has given you.

274

Peace That Passes Understanding

Philippians 4:6; 2 Corinthians 12:9; Isaiah 43:2; Jeremiah 32:17

May the peace that passes all understanding be yours today to guard your heart and mind from the busyness, conflicts, loss, and hurts that this world has to offer. May God's strength be made perfect in your weakness today. In all that you don't understand, may you humbly tell your Father what you don't know and what is hard for you to accept. Then let Him carry your burdens. With boldness may you declare what you know to be true, in spite of what your feelings may try to hide from you.

May you pause today and let God's supernatural power minister to you and through you. May you allow Him to speak comfort and strength, confidence and determination, acceptance and love into the spaces of your not now, not yet, wait, and it wasn't to be. May you feel His redirection from the "what ifs" and "could haves, would haves, should haves" into the "what is" and the surety that you are in the palm of His hands—exactly where you're supposed to be.

May you hear God's whisper reminding you that He is with you. Always. Trust Him. Be still in His strong embrace. God is very much in control. When you go through the water, He is with you. When you go through the river, it will not sweep over you. When you go through the fire, you will not be burned. He knows what you need today and will do everything to make sure you get it. He who made the heavens and earth by His great power can do everything and anything for you. Nothing is too difficult for Him. He loves you.

275

Something Extraordinary

Psalm 20:4–6, 21:2, 119:15; Joshua 1:8; Matthew 6:10

May something extra happen in your ordinary today to make it an extraordinary day! In your mundane routine, may you find many treasures. May you find God at work with you today—walking and talking with you, clearing the obstacles, opening the doors He wants you to walk through, answering your prayers before you even utter them, granting the requests of your lips. May your heart be sensitive to the things that move God, and your ears be tuned to His voice. May you meditate on and walk in so much truth that the devil's schemes fool only the deceiver himself and not you. May you partner with God today to accomplish kingdom-building in your life and through your life. May His kingdom come and His will he done on earth as it is in heaven.

276

Joy and Favour

James 1:2; Nehemiah 8:10; Psalm 1:1–3, 119:11; Proverbs 9:10, 10:22; Luke 2:52

May you choose joy today so that you can have strength. Joy and pain, sunshine and rain will be part of your life. God has planted seeds of greatness in your heart. They need the sun and the rain to produce fruit. May you be singing in the rain because of the joy that is down in your heart to stay. May your mind be stayed on Jesus so that you will be kept in perfect peace. May you pray with big belief that your big God is truly bigger than your problems because … He is! God is infinitely greater than the greatest problem you face. His grace is greater than the greatest sin in your life. There is no limit to God's greatness.

Today may God's Word that is hidden in your heart be on your mind and on your lips to keep you from sin and to produce fruit. May you fear the Lord and find knowledge and wisdom. May you grow in favour with the Lord and with people today, wherever you go and whatever you do. The favour of the Lord brings blessing, and no trouble is added to it. Blessed are you whose delight is in the law of Lord. As you are watered and your roots grow deeper, may you love the fruit that is being produced in you. May whatever you do prosper all for God's glory.

277

Covered in Love

Romans 8:38–39, 12:2; Jeremiah 31:3; Ephesians 3:17–19; John 15:4

May your life today be covered in the truth that nothing can separate you from the love of God in Christ Jesus. May you experience an expression of God's love everywhere you go and everywhere you turn. May you know that whether you are high on the mountaintop or in a low valley or somewhere in between, God's love has gone before you, is behind you, and is with you always.

May God show you how wide, long, high, and deep is His love. May you experience the relentless pursuit of His unconditional love. There is nowhere you can go that isn't in the presence of God. May you honour God today by acknowledging and enjoying His presence. May you serve Him well today. May you grow in Him and make your vine connection stronger as you abide in Him. May you know your value and worth because of who God says you are and because of His thoughts toward you. May God's truth be heard by you today. May God's revelation of Himself be seen by you today. May God's perfect will be done in your life today— nothing more, nothing less, nothing else.

278

Your Anchor

Hebrews 6:19, 13:8; 2 Corinthians 1:20; Psalm 91:1

May God's Word be the anchor that holds in every storm. May you live fearlessly and with boldness through frightening times because you know who holds the keys of victory. May the truth of knowing who Christ is, what He has done already, and what He will do empower you to keep going. Jesus is the same yesterday, today, and forever! Victory in Jesus isn't just for the future. Victory in Jesus is your present, your now, your reality forever.

As God reveals Himself to you in each moment, may you arise with fresh hope and confidence. Because He lives, you can face tomorrow. May you remember that when God has called you and says something is for you, it is. He is right. His Word is true. He is the Yes and Amen. Believe it. Nothing can stop you. No one can stop you from moving forward.

May you approach God's throne of grace and mercy to obtain any help you need. Do it with boldness. He is waiting for you. He is waiting for your belief. He is waiting for your request. He is waiting for your submission. He is waiting for you to let Him be who He already is— God. He has so much grace and mercy. He has an unlimited supply of love. He has it all to give to you. Let the winds blow. Let the rains fall. Let the heat rise. Nothing will keep God from showing His power on your behalf. Rest in the shadow of the Almighty. Stand still. Stand firm. He is your anchor.

279

Way of Truth

Psalm 119:1–48; 2 Chronicles 20:3, 12, 15, 20

May you choose the way of truth today. May your heart believe truth and your mouth declare it. Blessed are you who keep His ways and seek God with all your heart. May you live according to God's Word and keep your way pure. May God open your eyes to see wonderful things in His Word. May you see the good God is doing for you and in you. May you be preserved according to God's Word. May you be strengthened according to God's Word. May God give you wisdom and understanding and direct you according to His Word. May your spiritual eyes be opened to see the truth of what you are living in the physical realm.

With truth from God's Word, may you be able to answer those who taunt you. May you walk in the freedom that God gives to you. May you stand firmly, trusting God to fight your battles for you because He said He would. When the enemy tries to come at you, may you resolve to inquire of the Lord what your battle plan should be. Keep your eyes on Him when you don't know what to do. He always has an answer. The battle is not yours but God's. Have faith in God, and you will be successful.

280

Faithful Growth

Philippians 2:13, 4:6–7; 2 Chronicles 16:9

May the peace of God that passes all understanding be your experience today! May you be anxious about nothing but in everything, by prayer and supplication, with thanksgiving, make your requests to God. May you see God's grand plans unfolding before you, even through the challenges you might experience along the way. May you talk yourself out of doubting God and talk yourself into doing all that He has planned for you to do and be. May you see yourself growing into the person God destined you to be even before you meet your destination.

May you trust God as you climb mountains and find that although they may not get smaller, the climb is easier with Him as your companion. May your plans be secondary to His purposes. His ways are best. It is God who works in you to will and to act to fulfill His good purpose. May you see the move of God as He roams the earth looking to see who is committed to Him. And may you rejoice as He blesses you with strength because He has found you faithful.

281

Taste and See

Psalm 34:8; Colossians 2:10; Proverbs 3:5–6; Romans 13:8; John 15:12; Matthew 6:13; Isaiah 55:11

May you taste and see that the Lord is good today. May your moments with God be refreshing. May time spent with Him be the most satisfying thing you do today. May you know that you are complete in Him. May you trust in the Lord with all your heart. When you don't understand, lean on Him and His truth. In everything you do, acknowledge who is in control and you will find your way. You will be given clear direction.

May you keep His commandments and abide in His love. May you know how much you are loved and forgiven so that you can freely love and forgive others. You have been liberated. Through love, serve others in that freedom. May what you possess in Christ grow in you and be shared with others. May your eyes be open to God at work all around, and may you marvel at the glory that is being revealed to you.

Walk in faith today. Walk in boldness. Walk declaring, "Thine is the kingdom, the power, and the glory forever" and forever see that reality unfolding in your circumstances. May His kingdom come and His will be done on earth in your life as it has already been declared in heaven. What He has said to you and for you will come to pass. His Word does not return void. It accomplishes what it is sent to do. Believe it. Believe Him.

282

The Mind of Christ

Romans 8:6; John 10:10; 1 John 1:7; Matthew 27:37–40;
Psalm 23:6, 118:1, 24

May the mind of Christ dwell in you richly. May you be spiritually minded that you might experience a peaceful life. May you walk with Jesus, who has come to you that you might have life—abundant life. Walk in the light with Him and have good fellowship with those the Lord puts in your path.

May you love the Lord your God with all your soul, mind, and strength and your neighbour as yourself. Love is the greatest commandment. Receive His unconditional love and let it flow freely from your life. May you recognize your two companions who are always with you: goodness and mercy. Walk closely with them and share them with others. May you rejoice in this day. The Lord has made it. It is already perfect because it comes from your perfect God. He has already been good to you. From the rising to the setting of the sun, His faithfulness is great in your life. Give thanks to the Lord. His love endures forever.

283

Listen and Follow

Hebrews 11:6; John 15:11; Ephesians 3:16; Psalm 16:11;
Isaiah 30:21, 41:10

May you follow directions from the one who knows the way that is best for you to travel. May you listen carefully to the instructions of the one who always knows the what, the when, and the how in your life. May you pray prayers that make you scared and brave at the same time. You are a powerful praying saint. You are accepted in the king's court, and He rewards you for diligently seeking Him.

May your voice be filled with bold messages. May you be excited about being chosen to be used by God to be light in this dark world. May the Lord clear from your path anything that obstructs your view of Him. May He remove anything in your life that has replaced Him as your first love. May you rest in Jesus so you can rise in His strength. May you have more reasons to trust God than to live in fear. May you have more reasons to choose faith rather than doubt. May joy keep feeding you courage. It is the Lord's joy in you, and it makes you complete—completely strong, completely safe, completely confident, completely equipped to do and be all God has called you to.

May God strengthen you with power in your inner being out of His glorious riches. In His presence your joy is full, and there you hear Him whisper, "Fear not, for I am with you; be not dismayed, for I am your God. I will strengthen you, Yes, I will help you, I will uphold you with My righteous right hand. This is the way. Walk in it." Go forward in confidence wherever the Lord leads you today. He knows where you are going, and He is with you.

284

The Impossible Made Possible

Jeremiah 32:17; Luke 1:37; Genesis 18:14; Exodus 3:14;
John 6:35, 8:12, 10:11, 11:25, 14:6, 15:1

May you be reminded today that nothing is impossible with God. May you hear God ask "Is anything too hard for the Lord?" and be able to answer in faith that all things are possible with God. May your faith have substance today. May you place all your hopes before God as you place all your hope in God.

As you hear yourself say "I'm not sure about tomorrow," hear God say "I Am." As you cry "I'm not able to carry this load," hear God say "I Am." As you confess "I'm not who I thought I was or want to be," hear God say "I Am." As you debate with God that you're not able to start or have enough in you to finish, may you hear Him say "I Am. I Am the first and the last, the beginning and the end. I am who I am."

Do you need clarity, direction, access, provision, something to hold on to, a future? Whatever you need you have in Him. Listen to Him remind you of who He is and be strengthened. "I am the way, the truth, and the life. I am the light of the world. I am the good shepherd. I am the vine. I am the bread of life. I am the resurrection and the life. I Am all you need."

285

The Lord Is Near

Colossians 3:16; 2 Corinthians 12:9; Jeremiah 8:10; Hebrews 12:15;
Psalm 51:10; Romans 8:28; Philippians 4:4–9

May the word of Christ dwell richly within you. May you speak of the goodness of God. May you boast in your troubles, not because you're happy about having them, but because the Lord is near. He is with you, and His power is being revealed. It rests on you. His strength is made perfect, and His joy gives you more than you thought you had or was possible.

May the Lord restore to you the joy of His salvation, and may your heart cancel out the root of any bitterness. He is with you. May you see and believe that He is working every circumstance for your good. Rejoice in the Lord. He dwells in your praises. Pray about everything and be thankful that God hears and answer with a supernatural peace. Think about your true and noble God, who is always right and pure—perfectly holy.

He makes you lovely and admirable because you look to Him and are never covered in shame. He is the king, and His rule has no end. You are His. Think about Him. Think about His excellence and praise Him. Think about what He says to be true about you. Think about His Word and let Him carry you to a spacious place of freedom. It's in your DNA. Freedom is already yours. Take it. Breathe it. Live it.

286

Faith Expressed

Galatians 5:6; Mark 12:31; Psalm 37:5, 119:57, 58, 72;
2 Corinthians 12:9; Ephesians 2:10; 1 Peter 4:16

May your faith express itself through love today. May you love yourself and see what God sees in you. May you love others as you love yourself. God has made you to be a blessing. God will do in you and through you all He has purposed and planned as you commit your way to Him. You will find success in your commitment and obedience. His power is at work in you. His strength is made perfect in your weakness. May you advance in the good work that God created in advance for you to do.

May you walk in pride of living for Christ. Do not be ashamed of bearing His name but glorify God in all you do. May the Lord be your portion today. May you seek Him with all your heart and find His grace extended to you, just as He promised. May God's truth be more precious to you than anything—silver, gold, or anything this world can offer. May you put your hope in His Word and experience life-giving power in all you do today.

287

Awake with Expectation

Nehemiah 8; Isaiah 40:29; John 4:10, 6:36, 7:38; Psalm 34:10;
Matthew 5:6; Luke 4:4

May you awake with expectation and anticipation for what God has planned for you today. As you look at all of creation praising God with the vibrant colour of the flowers, the cozy warmth of the sun, and the coolness of the wind, may your heart overflow with joy and praises for the goodness and greatness of God. The joy of the Lord is your strength.

In your spaces and places of weakness, God has more than enough for you. He gives power to the weak, and for those who have no might He increases strength. Drink today and quench your thirst. He is your source of refreshment. He is the living water, and His well will never run dry. Rivers of living water will flow from within you as you continue to walk in belief.

Seek the Lord with all your heart. Taste and see that He is good. Your hunger will be satisfied and your appetite filled. Blessed are those who hunger and thirst for righteousness, for they will be filled. He is your bread of life. Go to Him and you will never go hungry. Keep going. Don't stop. His Word is life. You live by every word that proceeds from God's mouth. So eat, drink, and be merry in your Lord today. The table is set for you. Enjoy.

288

Choose Faith over Fear

Deuteronomy 31:8; Isaiah 45:2; Jeremiah 29:11; Psalm 139:17;
James 1:17

May you make a choice to "faith it" till you make it. In every challenging circumstance, may you believe God's Word above everyone else. May you trust that God is walking before you and clearing the way. May you walk with boldness because you approached His throne with boldness and have received the grace you need to keep going. May you remember that every good and perfect gift comes from God, and His intentions toward you are only good. May God's Word build your faith as you listen closely to His message. Trust Him when He says do not fear. He is with you and will never leave you.

289

Live Available

John 20:21; Ephesians 6:20–21; Joshua 1:9; Matthew 6

Today may your relationship with Jesus be about His will and not your wants. May you make yourself available to what and where God has placed you. As the Father sent Jesus, your Saviour is sending you forth to be His light and express His power. May you choose to make a difference. Wherever God sends you, may you ask Him to give you all you need to fearlessly proclaim Him. Be strong and courageous, for the Lord your God will be with you wherever you go.

May God open your eyes to who you can bless today. May He reveal to you the many blessings He is sending to you. May your ears clearly hear His message for you this day. Don't worry about tomorrow but know that your heavenly Father has everything taken care of. He knows what you need. Live in the day you have been given. Live in faith. Live in joy. Live in peace.

290

Give God Your Heart

1 John 4:4; Romans 8:37; Hebrews 11:6; Deuteronomy 32:4; Isaiah 55:9

May you experience deep in your heart the intimate touch of healing and strength from God, who loves you very much. May God meet you in the places of your disappointments and pain with gifts of encouragement and peace as He dries your tears and carries you to the place of divine appointment with Him. Open your heart to Him and don't allow anyone or anything else to have first place. He will fill it with His love and truth. Guard your heart, for it is the wellspring of life.

God will bring healing, and you will overcome. You are more than a conqueror through Him who loves you. Greater is He in you than he in the world. Your hope is not in vain. Keep the faith. You are pleasing God. He will keep His promises. God is strong enough and faithful. Stand strong in Him and His Word. He is a rock. He is perfect in all of His ways. God is thinking about you. He knows your future. His ways are higher. Trust the one who is above all things.

291

Stay Hopeful

Numbers 23:19; Hebrews 11:1; Jeremiah 29:11; Romans 12:12;
Psalm 33:18, 71:14

May you wake up today to fulfilled promises. The God you serve is a man of His Word. He does not lie. What He has spoken that He does, and what He promises comes to pass. May your hope be renewed because your eyes have been opened once again to fresh truth and you have chosen faith. Faith is the substance of things hoped for, the assurance of things not seen.

May you have fresh perspective about who God is and where He is leading you. He knows the plans He has for you—plans to prosper you and not harm you, plans to give you a hope and future. He is moving you forward. As you hope for more answers, stay joyful. As you work through challenges, be patient. God isn't finished with you. Remain faithful in prayer. He is listening. Always have hope and praise the Lord more and more. His eyes are on you because your hope is in His unfailing love.

292

Praise Him in the Storm

Isaiah 43:2, 61:1–3; Jeremiah 30:16–22

May you lift your hands and open your mouth in worship and find that you have renewed power as you praise Him through each circumstance. May the Spirit of the Lord be upon you, and may your life message today be one of good news. May you speak messages of healing to the broken-hearted, including yourself. May your song of praise and God's words of truth spoken from your lips proclaim freedom and shine light in the darkness. May God crown you with beauty for ashes and anoint you with the oil of joy instead of mourning. May you wear the garment of praise and walk away from heaviness. You are strong. You are planted in the Lord, and your roots grow deep. You will withstand the storm. You are planted where you are by the Lord, and you will display His splendour.

When you pass through the waters, may you look and see the strong one who goes with you. When you pass through the rivers, may you experience His hand of protection and see that they will not sweep over you. When you walk through the fire, may you see like Daniel that there is no scent on you—you will not be burned; the flames will not set you ablaze. The Lord is your shield. May songs of thanksgiving and the sound of rejoicing be heard from you as you reach your place of victory and look back and see that your enemies are no more. May there be much dancing as you testify that God has taken you to a place of safety, just like He promised. May you continually speak of God's restoration and rebuilding. Never stop telling of His faithfulness. He has never left you. He has been there all the time. He brings you honour. You are His. He is your God.

293

Take a Bold Approach

Hebrew 4:16; Ephesians 3:20; 1 Thessalonians 5:17; Matthew 6:11, 7:7;
Jeremiah 29:13; John 14:6; Isaiah 55:11; Numbers 23:19;
Psalms 16:2, 46:10, 62:1; Lamentations 3:24

You tell me that I can boldly approach your throne of grace and mercy to obtain help in my time of need. Here I am. I know that you are great. Only you can do exceedingly, abundantly more than I can ask for, imagine, or think. Lord, you have told me to pray without ceasing. Thank you that I can feel confident in coming before you again and again. I know that only you can answer me. I desperately need your will to be done in my life. I submit to you. Your kingdom come. Your will be done on earth as it is in heaven.

Lord, I am seeking you. You have promised that I will find you when I search for you with all my heart. I ask you because I only want you to answer. I am trusting your Word, which says to ask and it shall be given. I am seeking you. Your Word is true. You told me to seek and I will find. I will be persistent. I will not give up. I'm at the right door. I know this. You are the way, the truth, and the life. You have given me permission to knock and told me the door will be open. Your Word goes forth and accomplishes what you say. Speak your truth into my life. You are not a man to lie and change your mind. I believe you. I trust you. My soul finds rest in God alone. I will be still and know you are God. You will be exalted in the earth and in my life. I wait on you, Lord. You are my portion. I will wait on you. Apart from you, I have no good thing.

294

Keep Your Eyes Lifted

Psalm 34:8, 121:1–3; Hebrews 12:2; Philippians 1:6; Proverbs 3:5;
Ephesians 3:14–20

Dear Lord, I lift my eyes up to see you, as I know that you are where my help comes from. May you help me to keep my eyes on you so that I may see that you are bigger than my challenges. May I see your greatness and not my circumstances. You do not sleep, and you will keep me from slipping. May I taste and see that you are good. You are good for my strength, good for my hope, good for this moment and for my future. I am blessed as I take refuge in you. May you help me to keep my eyes on Jesus, the author and finisher of my faith.

You are faithful and will complete the work that you have started in me. Lord, I trust you with all my heart. Help me to lean on you and not my own understanding. In everything I do, I choose to acknowledge you as the one in control and trust the path you are leading me on. Lord, I pray that you will continue to strengthen me inside my heart and spirit with your power out of your glorious riches. May you dwell with me as I choose faith. May I be rooted and established in your love beyond my own understanding. May I grasp how high, wide, long, and deep your love is for me. I want your love to overwhelm me. May the fullness of God fill my life.

Lord, I give you glory because your power is at work in me. Thank you for doing immeasurably more than I can ask and imagine. Your name be praised. I worship and glorify you! Thine is the kingdom, the power, and the glory forever and ever. Amen.

295

Drown Out the Noise

John 10:27, 14:6; Psalm 5:8, 31:3, 32:8; Isaiah 45:2

May the noise and traffic around you be drowned out by the clear, direct voice of God. May your compass be set to the True North. Jesus is your North Star. If you want to reach the right destination, in the right way, may you follow the right path. May your prayer be "Lead me in the right path, Lord." May your choices be evidence that you have followed the right map and tour guide.

Only God and His Word will lead you forward. He goes before you and makes the crooked places straight. When you feel lost and unsure of your next step, remember that God is with you and orders your steps. Stop. Listen. Look up. He makes known the path of life, and His Spirit will lead you on level ground. He will guide you along the right path for His name's sake. He is the way, the truth, and the life. Follow Him and live.

296

Know and Believe His Love

Ephesians 3:18; 1 Peter 2:9

May you know and believe how much you are loved by God. May the truth of how wide, long, high, and deep the love of Christ is draw you closer into His arms. You can't escape it. He went to great lengths to show you His everlasting love. May you be defined by who God says you are and not by your mistakes and failures. May you live God's best life for you and nothing less.

May the love you have for God and the love He has poured into your life flow easily and in abundance to others who come into contact with you. May your prayers be the answer to someone else's prayers. May you know that your life is not an island unto itself but that you are connected to the big family of God. May the promises of God strengthen and encourage you. May they be enough for you today! Remind yourself of whose you are and who you are in Him.

297

Father, Open My Eyes to Your Love

Psalm 36:5–10, 108:4; Isaiah 41:13

May your heavenly Father open your eyes to His immeasurable, overflowing, never-ending supply of love that He extends to you always. May you climb up into His lap and stay in the comfort of His embrace today. As you pray Abba Father—daddy—may the kiss of His Spirit tenderly minister to your heart in powerful and practical ways as you need. May you know the pride that your heavenly Father feels toward you. He thinks about you all the time and is pleased with you. He delights in you, and you bring joy to His heart. May you hold on to His hand and know that He is holding on to yours. You are His.

298

Be Like Esther

Esther 4:14; Joshua 24:2, 15; Matthew 28:19–20; Luke 10:27; Micah 6:8

May you be like Esther, so desperate for God to move that you take bold and courageous steps because you know that you were created for such a time as this. What you do today can change the course of history! May you stand with certainty and declare like Joshua that "As for me and my house, we will serve the Lord." May you walk in obedience, going to where God calls you to the ends of the earth to make disciples. May you love the Lord your God with every part of your being—your heart, mind, soul ... all His—and love your neighbour as if she were you. Give her your best, choose the best for her, speak for her, put her first. May God's heart be what is exposed as you love mercy, act justly, and walk in humility with your God.

299

God's Word in Your Heart

Psalm 119:11; 2 Timothy 2:20–21, 3:16; Hebrews 4:12;
1 Samuel 15:22; 2 Corinthians 7:9–10; Isaiah 64:8

May God's Word have His way in your heart today. As you read, may it melt and mold, fill and instruct you in the way you should go today. May it show you more of God's heart and be a mirror of your own. May the changes that need to be made in your heart be revealed and addressed. Obedience is better than sacrifice.

Don't be afraid or ashamed. God works in you not to condemn but to convict unto repentance, that you might have life and be made into His image. He loves you so much and wants to continue to shape you into His masterpiece. God plans on using you and doing great things for His glory through you. He is making you strong and ready. Let His Word and truth have their way so that you can move in freedom and power.

300

His Words, Your Words

Ezekiel 37; Proverbs 3:5–6; Mark 11:23; Exodus 14:1

Today may His words be your prayers. As they are declared from your mouth, may you know that they do not return void. May your dry bones hear the Word of the Lord and come to life. May your heart believe His promises. Trust in Him with all your heart and do not lean on your own understanding. As you acknowledge Him in everything you do, He will make the paths in front of you straight.

May you speak to the mountains in your way and watch them tumble before you. May your dry bones hear the Word of the Lord and come to life. May you step forth into the sea that you are afraid of and watch Him part it for you as He delivers you from your enemies. You will walk on dry land because He is your firm foundation. You will look back and see that your enemies are no more. Sing unto the Lord because He triumphs valiantly. He goes with you to fight for you and give you victory.

301

Truth of Freedom

Galatians 5:1; Ephesians 6:10–17; John 8:36

Today may you know the truth of the freedom you have been given. It is for freedom that Christ has set you free. Stand firm and don't return again to the yokes that pull you to serve anyone else but Jesus. Stand firm against the devil's schemes. Stand firm, equipped in your armour. He has given you your belt, helmet, breastplate, shield, shoes, and sword. You have everything you need. Stand on His truth and in His power. He is your firm foundation.

Don't listen to voices that are contrary to the voice of Jesus. He is the only one with full authority. Don't listen to the voice of fear, doubt, division, unforgiveness, selfishness, defeat. Stand your ground! God has moved you to a higher place. He has declared you free. You answer to none but Jesus. He asks you to live in peace and unity. He asks you to follow Him, and although you take up your cross, you do it without chains. Your chains have been broken. There is nothing holding you back. You are free to run, dance, sing—to live for Him! Whom the Son sets free is free indeed! That is your truth!

302

God Breaking Through

Genesis 9:12–13; Psalm 73:26, 119:105; Ephesians 6:10

May you see a rainbow in your skies today breaking through the raindrops of tears that fall from your eyes and the clouds of doubt that try to darken your mind. May His Word shine light on your path and lighten the load you carry. God keeps His promises! May you stand tall today because you kneeled before Jesus. May you not get tripped up by little things, but may you climb high to joy and peace as you give thanks in everything. Look for the positive today, even in the challenges, and you will find God at work. Strengthen yourself in Him and speak of His faithfulness. He is the same yesterday, today, and forever. He is a good God and will never change.

303

Go with Jesus

Colossians 2:6, 4:6; 1 John 2:5–6; Hebrews 13:15; Isaiah 30:21;
Matthew 3:17

Wherever you go today, take Jesus with you. Take Him as your friend and walking partner. Take Him as your confidant and guide. Take Him as your support and strength. Whatever you say today, may your speech be seasoned with grace. May you encourage and build up. May you bring healing and help. May you speak truth. May you speak life. May you sing with joy and shout your praises. May the fruit of your lips give thanks.

Whatever you do today, may it be your best. May you know that you are equipped and capable. You can do all things through Christ, who gives you strength. Keep doing good. Don't give up or grow weary. You will see results and bear fruit. Whatever you see, may it be clear to you that God is at work and does all things well. May you look up and see His gaze of love and acceptance looking down on you. May you hear His voice saying "This is the way; walk in it. I am with you." May you hear Him say "You are mine. I am pleased with you, and I love you."

304

He Sees You

Jeremiah 23:24; Psalm 121, 46:1, 91:4; Proverbs 18:10; 2 Chronicles 16:9

May you not hide from the Lord but hide in Him. Heaven and earth are His. He fills all of heaven and earth. Nothing or no one can hide from Him. He sees you and knows where you are at all times. May He be your secret place, your shelter in the time of storm. He is your shield and rampart, your strong tower, your refuge and strength. Lift your eyes to Him. Your help comes from Him. He is for you and has everything you need. His eyes look throughout the earth to give strong support to you, who loves Him. Trust Him.

He will encourage you and strengthen you as you wait in Him and for Him to move on your behalf. Even when you can't see what God is doing, He never stops working. He doesn't slumber or sleep but keeps His protective eye on you and moves His hand to clear the way for you. His promises for you are true. He sees you. He hears you. He is the same yesterday, today, and forever, and He will never leave you. You have nothing and no one to fear. Keep taking your steps of faith. With each step you please God and live in victory.

305

God's Never-Ending Love

Jeremiah 31:3; Matthew 18:12; Genesis 50:20; Isaiah 54:17

May the overwhelming, ongoing, far-reaching love of God hold on to you today in a new way. May you run toward Him and not away from Him. If you stray and lose your way, may you know that He will chase after you. He loves you so much. Through the storms, may you be like the trees that do their dance in the wind, swaying but staying confidently rooted in Him.

May your arms reach to the sky, and your face turn toward the Son. May His Word water and refresh you and keep you firmly planted. May you know who you are because you know whose you are. You are the child of the King! You are blessed and highly favoured. May what was intended for evil in your life become a distant memory as you witness God turn it around for good. No weapon formed against you shall prosper, and every tongue that rises up with insult and deception will be condemned. You are covered and protected. The battle may come, but you are already and always a winner. The overwhelming, never-ending love of God will never let you go.

306

Rest

Luke 10:39; Psalm 63:4; 2 Peter 3:9; John 14:8

May you rest today in the arms of the one who loves you most. May you sit at the feet of Jesus and choose the most important thing. Many things will ask for your attention, but may you choose the one thing that is better and will not be taken from you. May you be like a child, enjoying His presence and waiting in expectation for good things. May you let go of what worries you so that you can hold on to all that your Father wants to give you. May you release your grip on what doesn't serve you so that you can raise your arms and open your hands in free worship and praise.

May you be replenished and refreshed, revived and rejuvenated, refocused and restored as you open your heart to the gifts God has to give you today. God hasn't forgotten His promise or purity, justness or holiness. He hasn't forgotten to act or move. He is patient and long-suffering and not willing to lose anyone ... even us. He is waiting in love for many to know Him, for others to obey Him, and for most to love Him above all else. Move closer to your faithful, loving God today. You will find all you need in His presence.

307

God's Good Plans

Revelation 3:7; Psalm 138:8; John 15:5; Isaiah 43:19

May your eyes be open to the new beginnings that are before you. May you be optimistic about each fresh start. May you be excited about the opportunities the Lord allows you to experience. May you walk through the doors that God's hand holds open for you and which no one can shut. The Lord will perfect all that concerns you. He does not forget the work of His hands. He is melting you and molding you. He is filling you and using you. He has set you apart. You are chosen. Abide in Him and Him in you. Enjoy that connection. You will bear amazing fruit and do amazing things as you stay connected. Apart from Him you can do nothing.

Trust Him. His plans for you are good. He is doing a new thing for you and in you. Do you not see it? Isn't the expectation great? He is making a way where you have wandered in the wilderness and in the dry spaces. The water is coming. You will be refreshed. Fountains of living water are about to be released in you. Open your eyes. See it. Believe it.

308

Sweet Hush

Acts 17:28; Psalm 46:10; Hebrews 4:16, 12:2

May you arise with thanksgiving for this present moment, which is your gift today. May you be aware of the many gifts present in each moment. With each breath you take, may you be more in awe of the miracle you are living. In Him you move and breathe and have your being. You are fulfilling purpose. Take some time to be. Be in His presence. Be still. In the rush, may there be a hush. May you sit at His feet and know you have chosen right. You are redeeming the time. There is no waste there.

May you approach your Father with confidence, knowing that the one who is in charge of the universe is mindful of you. He knows your name. He knows your thoughts. He sees each tear and hears your voice call out to Him. He is drawing you into His arms and heart. He is the potter and you are the clay. He is interested in who you are becoming more than anything you are doing or will ever do. His internal work in your heart and mind is the masterpiece. Look unto Jesus, the author and finisher of your faith. He is writing His story of faithfulness through you. Today is a new day to love and be loved as you live in Him.

309

Mind of Christ

Colossians 3:16; Romans 12:2; Joshua 1:8; Isaiah 30:21

May the mind of Christ be yours today. May His words richly dwell within your heart so that they may flow freely from your lips and bring life, wholeness, and healing. May your thoughts be His thoughts. Let your patterns and choices be transformed by the renewing of your mind so that you will know with confidence God's good, pleasing, and perfect will. May you meditate on God's truth and be careful to live by it so that you may prosper and have success in all you do. God's Word will ground you. His promises will lead you. His truth will strengthen you. His followed plans and purpose are best. His way is the way of freedom. May you hear Him guide and direct you. May you hear His voice clearly as He says "This is the way; walk in it." As you abide in Him, and His Word in you, you will bear fruit. Be fruitful today and multiply His blessings and kingdom.

310

Stay in the Race

Hebrews 11:6, 12:1–3; James 1:4

May choices of risk today be steps of obedience. It's all about having the right perspective. Keep your eyes on Jesus, the only one who rewards you well when you diligently seek Him. May you step away from fear and step out in faith. It's the only way to see God. May every test cause you to run into the arms of the one who can give you a testimony. May you release bitterness and become better with every challenge you face. May you allow problems to gracefully break you and make you into the person God has intended for you to rise into.

May perseverance finish its work in you so that you may be complete and lack nothing in who you are to be and what you are to do. Keep going. Run the race marked out for you. Run in the path of God's command and broaden your understanding of who He is and the amazing things God can do. Follow in His ways and you will finish well. In all your ways acknowledge Him and He will direct your paths. You will never go wrong looking to the one who is right and perfect in all of His ways.

311

Enough

Psalm 139:13–14; Isaiah 64:8; Ephesians 2:10; Esther 4:14;
James 1:17; 1 Peter 4:10

Today may you know that no matter what, you are enough. Everything you are is who God made you to be. You are enough for the task. You are enough for the moment. You are enough for the position. You were created for such a time as this. May you know that everything you are and have has been given to you by God. His gifts are good. He makes no mistakes. May you continue pursuing your dreams with a fire and passion fuelled by the power of God in you.

You are enough because God is enough. Let nothing stop you. Fight for what God has put in your heart and confirmed in your spirit. May you see your mistakes as an opportunity for growth and never give up. May you experience the moments of waiting as moments of strengthening and character building. Keep believing. Keep hoping. Keep praying. The wait is making the achievement more glorious. All that God has for you is yours. Do not worry. God isn't worried. Rest in Him and trust Him to be more than enough for you.

312

Trust

2 Corinthians 1:20; Joshua 23:14; 1 Kings 8:56; Deuteronomy 28:1–14

May you be infused with fresh hope in believing that God is a man of His Word. If He said it, you can believe it! He is not a man that He should lie. He does not change His mind. What He has spoken, He will do. All He promised will come to pass.

You are blessed in the city and the field. You are blessed in your going and coming. You have been given authority to cast down every stronghold that tries to take a hold of you. Sickness and poverty cannot advance their purposes! The enemy has been defeated. There is power in the name of Jesus to break every chain. Put on your armour. You have been given the strongest battle gear. Wear it proudly. Wear it properly. Stand firm in it. Stand firm against the devil's schemes. Know your truth! Be courageous! Be strong! See what God is doing and will continue to do for you! You are blessed!

313

God Surprise

Psalm 91, 27:14; Ephesians 1:17

May God surprise you with expressions of His love today. Wait and look for it with expectation and anticipation. May there be fresh revelation of His presence and power in places and moments you least expect it. May God answer prayers you didn't pray but so desperately needed answered. May you be encouraged today as God continually works on your behalf, showering you with His protection and provision, His defence and deliverance. He is all you need and more.

314

Anchor Holds

Hebrews 6:19; Mark 4:35–41; Matthew 14:22–33

May your anchor hold in spite of the storm. May you look and see Jesus in the boat with you. Yes, He may be asleep, because He knows where He's taking you and that you'll reach your destination. He knows where you are going. He knows His power. He knows the power of His presence. He asks you to keep the faith. Listen closely as He whispers to your heart "Peace be still."

Be ready to step out of the boat. He will steady your feet as He calls you forward to walk on water. Keep your eyes on Him. Be brave. Watch and once again be amazed at how the winds and waves obey the sound of His voice. No storm is too hard for your Lord to navigate for you. He is in control. The sun will break through. The Son already has!

315

No More War

Revelation 17:14, 21:4; Isaiah 2:1–4; Acts 2:24; Zechariah 4:6

A s you pause to remember the sacrifice of so many, may you pause to remember love. May your memory of God's love and sacrifice remind you that He is still sovereign. May you hold on to the promise that He never leaves you or forsakes you. May your restless heart be calmed and your fears removed. May you be reminded that although the battle rages and wars arise, God has won the ultimate victory. His blood was shed for the past, present, and future. There will be a day of peace. The enemy's time is limited. Not by your might or power do you win today, or any day, but by the Spirit of the Lord. The Lord fights for you, and He always wins!

316

Persevere

Isaiah 4:6, 40:4, 61:3: Job 23:10

May God help you to persevere in climbing the mountain you are asked to climb. May He show you that He is your oasis and shade in the desert season. May you find shelter from the wind and rain in the deep valley, and may the waters that flow through them provide refreshment to your soul. May every season reveal in you your beauty, like the sight of gold or diamonds dug deep from the earth and coming out of the fire with great purity and value. Your life journey may not always make sense, but God is doing something. He is making beauty out of ashes. When He has tested and tried you, you will come forth like pure gold. No moment is wasted. Our good God is always doing something for your good and His glory.

317

May God Multiply

Jeremiah 30:19; Matthew 15:32–39; 2 Kings 4:1–7; Psalm 118:24

May the Lord multiply what little you have to offer Him today. May He give you a double portion of His joy, because that will be your strength. The joy of the Lord is your strength! Be strong in the Lord and in His power. Your God is mighty to save! May you see God do the miraculous through your sacrifice of praise. May you experience His amazing power do more with the limited loaves of bread and fish you freely give to Him, because your grateful heart knows that only God can. May your last jar of oil become your first jar of abundance. God is in the business of anointing and overflow. He has come that you might have life more abundantly. As you close your eyes in prayer, may you see in the spirit the great things God wants to reveal to you. When you open your eyes, may you see the amazing possibilities of this day that He has made and rejoice!

318

Share Brilliance

Daniel 12:3; Proverbs 4:18; Matthew 5:14–16; Ephesians 5:8

Just as the sun rose today sharing its brilliance of colour, and its rays began to reach far and shed light, may your life share its beauty and light on the path that you and others will walk today. May you be remembered as someone who made a difference in another's life today. May your potential in this day be emphasized and reached. May you be intentional in seeking truth and living in truth so that when you look back on today, you are looking forward into a destiny filled with hope and purpose.

God wants to accomplish so much through you for His purpose. Be confident in your submission to Him. Great things are about to happen, and you can be part of His plan when you say yes to His way. Go ahead. He is patiently waiting to give all you need. Oh, the places you will go!

319

Planted Firm

Jeremiah 17:7–8; Hebrews 13:15; Psalm 46:10

May you be like a tree planted by the water, firmly established and not moved by circumstance or storm because your roots are deep in the soil of God's Word and truth. May you be shade for someone as your arms are lifted heavenward. May the fruit of your lips give thanks and be refreshment to those in your path today. May whatever rain that falls water your soul so that you continue to grow into a beautiful tower of strength and beauty.

Joy and pain, sunshine and rain are all being used by God to accomplish His very best in your life. Be still and know that He is God. He will be exalted in the heavens. He will be exalted in the earth. He will be exalted in your life.

320

You Can Do It

1 Thessalonians 5:24; Psalm 138:8; Jeremiah 1:12; 2 Corinthians 9:8

Today may you find out about yourself what God already knows. Where you feel ill equipped or lack confidence, may you know that if God has called you, He will use what you have and do for you what you cannot. He has enough. He is enough. He will use you for His glory. God will fulfill His purposes and plans for your life. He is responsible for making His own words and promises come to pass. He who is faithful will do it. We are responsible for trusting Him.

We have the choice to submit. Will you exercise your faith today? His divine power has given you everything you need for life and godliness. Take what He has already given and continues to give and keep walking forward. God is able to make all grace abound to you so that in all things and at all times, having all that you need, you will abound in every good work. God has called you. He knows you can do it. Believe Him.

321

Bigger Plans

1 Corinthians 2:9; Isaiah 55:8–9; 2 Chronicles 16:9; Galatians 6:9; James 1:4

May you get a glimpse of the bigger plan God has for your life today. May you see that there is more than meets the eye. Things are not always as they appear. May your spiritual insight and vision be opened up and more of God's perspective be made known to you. Stay committed to Him because He is looking to bless you. He will show himself strong in your life. He keeps His word. His promises are yes and amen.

Do not grow weary in well doing because you will reap a harvest if you don't give up. Run your race and let His power and presence build your endurance. There are so many cheering you on. Persevere so that you will be complete and lack nothing. God's best is in store for you. There's always a greater plan. Always.

322

Lean in to God's Voice

John 10:27, 16:13; Psalm 86:16; Ephesians 3:18–19

Today as many voices call you to listen, may your ear lean in to the voice that tells you great truth. May you hear God telling you that you are chosen and not forsaken. May you hear God's voice tell you over and over again that you are who He says you are and nothing less. May you shut out every lie from the enemy and every other voice that does not align with God's. You are loved. You are created in His image. Your worth and value is defined by Him alone. May God's voice be crystal clear today. Build your life and hope in His truth alone. It is His breath in your lungs. Praise Him. Trust Him. Rest in Him.

323

God's Word, Your Lamp

Psalm 119:105; 2 Corinthians 5:7; Philippians 4:19; Ephesians 3:20–21

Today may God's Word be the lamp unto your feet and the light on your path. May His truth lead the way for you through open doors and give you new opportunities to share His love and power. Today when you feel like you don't have enough … enough strength … enough peace … enough joy … enough love … may God be enough … more than enough. Step out in faith to do and be. He supplies all your needs according to His riches in glory. Ask for what you need. He does exceedingly abundantly above all you can ask or imagine. Ask big! You can do all things through Christ. Believe in yourself. Believe in Him!

324

The Lord's Side

Joshua 5:13–15, 24:15; Ecclesiastes 10:2

May you choose to be on the Lord's side today. May your choices be for Him and not for anyone else. May everything you do be in response to His Word and voice. You will always be a blessing when you choose Jesus. You will always be a blessing following the lead of the Holy Spirit. With so many voices shouting for you to choose whose side you're on, may you hear His whisper asking you to choose the side of love, the side of forgiveness, the side of holiness, the side of the cross. May you confidently be able to say "I am not on your side. I am not on my side. I am on the Lord's side."

325

Find Rest in God Alone

Psalm 62, 46:1; John 16:33

In this season of unrest, may you be able to confidently say "My soul finds rest in God alone." May you run into His arms and know His power in quietness and trust. May you be still in the embrace of His strong arms and know that when you don't know what to do, your Father does. God has a plan. He remembers you. He sees you. God is your refuge and strength. He has not left you. He is a very present help in trouble. He is a shelter in a time of storm. Stay under the shadow of His wings. His angels have charge over you. You can be at peace, not because life is without trouble but because God is still in control. He is strong enough to carry you, protect you, defend you, deliver you, provide for you, heal you, and save you. Yes, God is still God.

326

A Heart of Gratitude

1 Thessalonians 5:18; Colossians 3:17; Isaiah 12:4–5; Psalm 9:1;
Matthew 6:26

May gratitude fill your heart and flow from your lips. May the gift of today remind you of so many other things to be thankful for in times when it can be easy to forget that God is at work. May you see how God continues to bless you in each moment. May you see how God continues to display His power in each moment. Greatness is His. Power and glory, victory and majesty all belong to Him. Everything in heaven and earth is His. May that truth allow you to move through your day singing "He's Got the Whole World in His Hands" and "Jesus Loves Me This I Know."

In His greatness He is mindful of you. You matter to God. You can sing because of His joy in your heart and because He has set you free. You can sing because He watches you. His eye is on the sparrow and on you too! He clothes the lilies and will certainly take care of your every need. You are His!

327

Abide

John 1:1, 15:4; Psalm 112:1; Matthew 15:28; Proverbs 30:5

May you abide in Him today. Walk with Him. Talk with Him. Listen to Him. Read His Word. Meditate on His Word. Speak His Word. Blessed is the one whose delight is in the Lord. Jesus is ready to touch you with His presence as you reach out to Him with yours. He is ready to respond to your faith. He is faithful to show you the way. He is faithful to show Himself strong. He is walking with you, yet He has gone before you. Oh, the mystery of His power.

He has a message for you. As you read His Word, may you know His heart. You are reading His love letter to you. Listen, even through your tears. Let His love and truth allow your spirit to hush as He tenderly ministers to you. Be still. He is still God. He always will be.

328

Remember, You Are Blessed

Deuteronomy 28; Psalm 37:5, 121:8; Genesis 12:2

As you move through your day, may you constantly be reminded that you are blessed. You woke up blessed. You are blessed where you live. You are blessed where you work. You are blessed in your going and coming. Sickness and poverty cease as you walk in your blessing. The devil is defeated because you are blessed with the victory in the cross.

You are blessed for a purpose. You are blessed to be a blessing. No matter what is happening around you, live in the truth of your blessing and be a blessing to others. Commit your ways to the Lord and you will be successful. Trust Him and He will do what needs to be done. The Lord has called you blessed, and that is your truth today.

329

Your Steps Are Ordered

Psalm 37:23; Proverbs 16:9; 2 Corinthians 5:7; Isaiah 26:3, 55:8–9

Today may you experience in a practical, tangible way what it means to have your steps ordered by God. May your choices today be in obedience to His leading. May the steps of faith you take today increase your trust in Him. In your places of uncertainty and fear, may you feel God's presence filling you with peace as you focus your mind on Him. He promises to keep you in perfect peace as your mind is stayed on Him. He promises that the peace of God that passes all understanding will guard your heart and mind as you make your requests to Him with thanksgiving. You can trust Him. Thank Him before the answers come because He is working on your behalf and knows what is best for you. His ways are higher, and He is always good. He will perfect all that concerns you. You can cast all your cares on Him because He can handle it all. Most importantly, He cares for you!

330

Revelation and Restoration

Psalm 119:18; Matthew 5:8, 6:10; Isaiah 40:31; Ephesians 1:17–19

May today be a day of revelation and restoration. As God reveals more of His truth to you today, may you make kingdom-building choices and not just ones that feel good to you. May you choose to speak to God and others about the injustices and hurts that are happening around you. May God restore your heart and your hope. May He restore your belief in miracles and healing.

May today be a day that the messages of life and beauty, of the promise of a victorious future, of God's power and provision and His rule and reign be the message that rings loud and takes root in your heart. May God open your eyes to His continued work in your life through the good and the bad. As your eyes are opened, may your faith increase. As you wait on the Lord today, may you run and not grow weary (in well doing), walk (with Him and toward Him) and not faint but soar like the eagle and have kingdom view and perspective. Let your kingdom come and will be done on earth, oh Lord.

331

Desire Him

Proverbs 2:1–5; Psalm 25:4–5, 119:151, 145:18; Matthew 6:21, 33

May you desire to lean in and hear God whisper His messages of love to you today. May you desire to spend time with Him and step away from the busyness of life. May you steal moments to create deeper intimacy with the one who loves you more than anyone else. God's love for you is unconditional and far reaching. He is calling out to you. He has rest waiting. He has strength waiting. He has joy and peace waiting for you. At any moment and in every moment, He is there to give you everything you need. Every good and perfect gift comes from Him. May being with Him be of more value to you than doing for Him today. And in the being, may He wash every tear, remove every doubt, and remind you that you are His and He is taking care of you. Today may your greatest gift be the power of His presence.

332

Move with Confidence

Ephesians 6:10; Philippians 4:13; Isaiah 55:11; Psalm 84:11

Today as you receive God's power, may you move with confidence in everything you do. May you be bold and courageous and step into new territory the Lord is giving you. May your eyes see the open doors you are to walk through. May your ears hear the voice of God leading your way. He has already spoken into this day, and His words do not return void. He is ordering your steps, and no good thing does He withhold from those who walk uprightly. Follow His lead. He is with you.

333

Operate in Freedom

2 Corinthians 3:17; John 8:32, 36; Galatians 5:1, 14; Romans 8:1–2

Today may you operate in the freedom that you have been given. May you live in it and enjoy it. You are free to run. Free to dance. Free to sing. Free to choose this day whom you will serve. Free to live for Jesus. Free to be generous. Free to be grateful. Free to extend compassion and mercy. You are free to pray. Free to praise. Free to ask for what you need. It is for freedom that Christ has set you free, no longer to be subjects to the yoke of slavery. You are free to live in victory. Free to love and be loved. Free to dream. Free to rest in God and know that He works all things together for your good because you love Him and He has a purpose for you. He has started a good work in you and will complete it. You are free to live in truth. Let nothing hold you back!

334

Expectation and Anticipation

Isaiah 42:9, 43:19, 65:17; Job 8:7; 1 John 4:18; Psalm 136:25

As you enter into this day, may you rise with expectation and anticipation that God is going to do a new thing. Whatever you are facing, may you know that God has gone ahead to make the crooked places straight. He is in control and does exceedingly abundantly above all you can ask or imagine. So ask big. Exercise your imagination. Then sit back and watch God surprise you. Remember that there is nothing too hard for the Lord. He keeps His covenant with you. He hears your prayers. Be bold in your prayers today. Be bold in your lament. Be bold in your trust and confidence. Be bold in your belief. Be bold in your hope. Be bold in your service. Be bold in your praise. Be bold in your testimony. You have nothing to be ashamed of. Do not fear. God loves you with an everlasting love. May you know that nothing can separate you from the love of God in Christ Jesus. Nothing! He who began a good work in you is going to complete it. He will never let you go. Expect to receive His love and power today. He is for you. He is with you.

335

Dressed

Philippians 4:6–8; Colossians 3:12–14, 17; Romans 13:14;
Ephesians 4:24

Today's a new day! As you awake to newness, may you continue to breathe in His grace and breathe out His praise. May you inhale peace and strength and exhale worry and fear. You have many choices to make today. As you get dressed and look in the mirror, may you see what God sees. May your reflection be the image of beauty God has created you to be. May you clothe yourself with the garments that honour God and bless others. Put on the garment of praise. Wear the pieces of compassion, kindness, humility, gentleness, patience, and self- control. Don't forget that you may travel into some unexpected, unsafe, and uncomfortable territory, so make sure you have your armour on. Wherever you go and whatever you do, know that God is with you, leading you. May your choice to follow God today take you to places you have never been before but places you will want to return to again. Enjoy your journey today. You're dressed for it. You look beautiful!

336

See God's Goodness

Psalm 100:1–5, 107:1; Romans 15:13

Today as you reflect on the goodness of God, may you see what He is doing right now before your eyes so that you don't miss the miracles of each moment. May you be blessed in so many ways by His expressions of love so that you can continue to be a blessing to many others. May your gratitude and thanksgiving rise up like a sweet fragrance into the atmosphere, causing everyone around you to be drawn into the joy and peace of contentment. May the God of hope fill you to overflowing with great expectation of what He is going to do next and how He is going to use you. God is on the move. Look, He is doing a new thing! You have every reason to be excited! Enjoy your day. You are blessed.

337

Expressions of His Love

Ephesians 3:20–21; Philippians 4:8

May God surprise you today with expressions of His love. May you experience Him doing exceedingly abundantly above all that you have asked or imagined as you focus your mind on His excellence. As you praise Him because He is worthy, may you dance in victory with joy and freedom. May your spirit rise in strength because you already know that God has amazing things in store for you! As you think on what is excellent and praiseworthy, may God open up your eyes in wonder to each moment of the miracle you are walking through today! He is doing a new thing!

338

Gifts Are Waiting

Matthew 11:28–30; Exodus 33:14; Psalm 34:8; Isaiah 58:11;
Lamentations 3:22–23; Zephaniah 3:17

Today as you rest in God, may you find all the gifts that are waiting just for you! May your soul be refreshed and your spirit rejuvenated. May you take time to drink from the well as much as you want and need, as the supply has no limit. May the table spread for you awaken all your senses and satisfy you more than you expected as you taste and see that the Lord is good. He has a new supply of mercy and compassion to extend to you. His faithfulness never fails. May you rejoice and sing and dance without shame before your God and others because of what He has done. This is your day! The gifts God has given you and the gifts you will continue to open are reason to celebrate. God is rejoicing over you. Join Him in the party! This is the day that He has made—let us rejoice and be glad in it!

339

Hope

Isaiah 9:7; Romans 5:3–5, 15:13; 1 Corinthians 2:9

May the God of hope expand yours by filling you to overflowing with His joy and peace. May each breath you take today remind you of the miracle of Christmas and the truth that God is not finished with you. He always has another plan. May your hopes and dreams for your future be confirmed by the carols that tell the story of God's promises kept and fulfilled. May your hope be renewed in the sounds, smells, visual beauty, and traditions of this season. Hope does not disappoint you. Hope is Jesus. He came. He has done what He came to do. He is coming again. You have every reason to hope. Christmas comes once a year, but Jesus is with you every day of every year. There is no end to His rule. There is no end to the hope you get to live in. God has prepared so much for you that is yet to be seen or heard. Keep hope alive!

340

Follow Closely

Psalm 16:11, 34:5; Matthew 22:37

As you walk with Jesus today, may you follow closely and treasure your intimate moments. He is showing you the path to take. He is your example. He is your lead. May you emulate the one who knows best. As you look to Him, the one you most admire, may He show you how to lead others to Him through the choices you make and the things you say. He has put you in a high position. You are blessed and highly favoured. There are many looking to you and following your lead. There are many who admire you. Show them whose you are and whom you believe. Show them that the joy of the Lord is your strength. Show them that your peace comes from keeping your mind stayed on Him. Show them that you love the Lord with all your soul, heart, mind, and strength and that He loves you unconditionally. As you walk with Jesus today, may every step of the way unfold blessings of answered prayers. He has already made the crooked places straight. He has ordered your steps. He is making you radiate a story of His faithfulness. Keep your eyes on Him and you will shine!

341

See the Beauty Revealed

Proverbs 4:18; Psalm 113:3; Jeremiah 31:5; Numbers 6:25

Today as the sun shines brightly and its rays shed light, may you open your eyes to the beauty of God that is being revealed in you and around you. May you be filled with pure joy. May you see your purpose and direction with pure clarity and radiate hope and peace. May what flows from your heart and mouth be as beautiful and pure as looking through a perfectly formed, crystal clear diamond. You are like pure gold. You have the highest value in the eyes of our Lord. You are the apple of His eye. Show the world you are worth more than the world dictates. Walk in His truth. Your life has meaning. You are a precious gift. He has gifted you with so much and in so many ways. Share your gifts and be a blessing. Be bold and see what God is going to do and say to others through the gift of you.

342

You Are Right Where You Should Be

Ephesians 2:10; Galatians 5:16; Isaiah 30:21, 41:10; John 16:13;
Psalm 119:105, 139:13–14

A s you walk with God today, may you know that you are right where He wants you to be. As you remember the love and sacrifice of Jesus, may you be reminded that you are in right standing, as you have been bought with a price. You are covered, and the righteousness of God is yours. May the Holy Spirit lead you into all truth and whisper to you that everything about who you are is right. You are fearfully and wonderfully made.

As you stand on His Word, walk with confidence that the steps you are taking are right because His Word is a lamp unto your feet and a light on your path. Go forward today trusting that you have heard His voice saying "This is the way … keep moving … you are right to follow me … I am right in front of you … I am leading you, my child … I will remain faithful … be bold and courageous … do not fear … I am with you."

343

Stand in Your Nobility

Romans 8:17; James 1:17; Philippians 4:19; Hebrews 4:16

May you stand in your nobility today. You are a child of the Most High. You are a child of the King of Kings. You are joint heirs with Jesus. Your Father is rich. Every good and perfect gift comes from Him. You have every spiritual blessing you need. Everything you need is in Him. Go ahead and ask Him, and He will supply according to His riches in glory.

He delights in hearing your requests and answering your prayers. He invites you to approach His throne with boldness in your time of need. For you, He gives His best! Nothing is too hard or too difficult. His provision is from a place of abundance. Today may you hold your head high with the crown He has placed on you. Wear your crown of favour with certainty that He sees you and delights in you. You are radiant. He loves what He sees. Adjust your crown. Let it sit right and comfortably! It is yours by right! You belong to the royal family of God.

344

Live in Truth

Psalm 139:17; James 1:5; Romans 11:33; Matthew 28:20; John 14:12

Today may you live in truth. May you know the truth of God's thoughts toward you. Thoughts of love and acceptance. Thoughts of joy and pride. Thoughts of compassion and mercy. May you know the truth of His Word and that He is generous toward you and will give you all the wisdom you need if you only ask. The depth of riches both of the wisdom and knowledge of God is too much for words. May that truth make you secure in the strength of your God. God is for you and will never leave you. May you walk in this truth today, knowing that you have a partner for life in this journey. Nothing is too difficult for your God. You know the truth of His power and promise, so rise in the freedom of this truth! You have been set free to walk in faith and to believe for great things!

345

God's Loving Embrace

Isaiah 41:10, 13, 49:16; John 10:29; Psalm 139:10; Zephaniah 3:17

May you be warmed today by God's loving embrace and be reminded that you are held tightly in His arms. May His strength take you to a safe place you thought you were too weak to get to. May you trust His voice as He whispers permission into your ears that you truly can rest in Him. May you hear Him loudly as He quiets you with His love. He is for you. He is with you. May you join Him in the song He sings as He rejoices over you. You are His and He is in your midst to do mighty things in and through you.

346

Love

Romans 8:35–39; Zephaniah 3:17; Ephesians 3:17–19;
2 Corinthians 9:15

May you wake up today to a thick blanket of love wrapped around you. May your spirit be warmed as you allow God's warm embrace to remind you that you are safe in His love. May God's song of love be the best music to your ears as you listen to songs of this season played over the airways. May you know beyond a shadow of a doubt that nothing can separate you from His love.

Love came down at Christmas and has never left you. You are always loved. You were loved from the beginning of time. You will be loved into eternity. May your heart receive His expression of love in a fresh way today. May the depth, height, breadth, and length of God reach you today and change your life. May you extend love to others in a new way. May love abound wherever you are. God is love and He is good. Thanks be to God for His indescribable gift that keeps on giving.

347

God's Song of Love

Psalm 104:12; Matthew 6:26, 10:31

As you hear the birds sing today, may God translate His song of love over you. May you feel the warmth of His breath whispering truth into your ears today, as real as the breeze that blows with the wind. As the rain falls, may your soul be freshly watered so that you may see that there is life in you to be lived. You have a purpose. May you dance with God today, following each step as he leads and resting in His arms as He reminds you that you are Daddy's beloved child. He loves you so much. May that reality fill you with peace, hope, and joy today and every day.

348

Courage

2 Corinthians 3:12; Hebrews 13:6; Acts 4:13; Luke 1:37;
Numbers 11:23; Isaiah 59:1; Ezekiel 37; Psalm 19:7–11

May you have courage to triumph over fear today. May you put fear in its rightful place. May you conquer fear by being brave enough to boldly step out in faith. May your boldness be a testament to others that you have been with and belong to Jesus. Impossible has never stopped God. You are God's child, a joint heir, so don't let impossible stop you. May you know that there is no limit to God's power. He doesn't run out of miracles! Speak to your dry and dead situations and let them hear the word of life from the Lord. When obedience and opportunity meet, God works miracles! May you do what God calls you to and watch Him do the miraculous. God is still amazing. God is still great. God is still and always will be God.

349

Find Refuge

Psalm 30:5, 35:18, 46:1, 56:8; Jeremiah 32:17

May you know that God already knows how much you need Him today. May you know that He collects your tears, and joy comes in the morning. May you rest in comfort because He is close to the broken-hearted. May you supernaturally feel Him holding and carrying you. May you supernaturally see what, where, and how God is using your circumstance to bring glory to His name by doing a work in you. May God reveal His power today in His touch in every realm of your experience and give you peace that passes understanding in your mind and emotions. May you thank God for walking with you. Thank Him for His presence and protection as you take refuge in Him.

350

Let Love Reign

Romans 13:8; 1 Peter 4:8; Psalm 91:1; 1 Corinthians 14:1;
Colossians 3:14–17

May you love deeply, freely, and lots today. It's the greatest gift you can give to anyone and everyone. May you value love and know that it is of greatest value. If you love, you have nothing else to give anyone that could be worth more. You have fulfilled the law by loving another person. May you know that it is love, God's love, that helps you forgive. It covers over a multitude of sins.

Love is not just a feeling. It's a choice. It's a covering and a place of safety. May you choose today to cover someone with love. May you choose today to be a safe place for someone. May you choose today to stay in the safety and under the covering of Jesus. Stay close to His heart. There is acceptance, strength, comfort, and joy there. He has enough love to pour into you and to flow through you. May you let love be your highest goal. May you let love bond everything together in your life today. All that seems loose is brought together with love. May you let love bring peace and unity. May you let love give you a new song of thankfulness and gratitude. Let love reign today.

351

Rise Up

Psalm 40:1–3, 73:23; 1 Peter 3:12; 1 John 3:1, 4:4; Nehemiah 8:10;
Philippians 4:4; Isaiah 40:29, 54:17; 2 Timothy 1:7

May you know that God sees and hears you. May you raise a shout of thanksgiving because you know that He holds you and carries you in His arms. May you grow in adoration of the one that loves you unconditionally and keeps His promise to never leave you alone. May gratitude fill your heart as you recognize His power in you. Greater is He in you than he in the world. May you give praise that no weapon formed against you shall prosper.

May you know where your power comes from. God and God alone has given power, love, and a sound mind! May the joy of the Lord continually be your strength. May you stand back and see God's strength made perfect in your weakness. May you rest confidently in God's power knowing that He knows exactly what you need. Let God touch your mind, emotions, body, and spirit with a supernatural touch. May you know that your attitude will raise you to a place of thriving above your circumstances. Be raised today in His power for His glory.

352

Be Still

Psalm 46:10; Hebrews 11:6; 1 Corinthians 2:9; Job 42:2

May you find strength, peace, joy, hope, healing, protection, wisdom, and direction in being still. There is no reward in rushing. There is no silver lining in stress. May you take your time to have your steps navigated by the one who moves in mysterious ways. We think we find our strength in doing, but we don't have to strive … we only tire ourselves out. He blesses us with strength when we are still.

May you know that the blessing of God Himself is greater and stronger than anything else. "Be still and know that I am God," He whispers. When life is filled with busyness and you can't keep up with the hustle and bustle, be still! When your mind is racing with too many thoughts and filled with clutter, be still! Don't just stop to hear yourself think. Stop to hear Him speak and to know that He is God! Take your time in God's presence. You don't have to fix your obstacles and challenges—God is already at work. You just have to find Him in them. Be still.

What takes you a lifetime only takes God a moment. Be still. Only He is God and expected to be great. Only He is God and expected to work miracles. Be still and let God's plans and promises unfold. You can't fathom or imagine what He is up to! He is the infinite God, and nothing can stop Him. May you know this truth: when you choose to stop worrying, fighting, doubting, and stressing, God is unstoppable.

353

Joy

Luke 10:9–10; Matthew 2:10; Psalm 118:24; John 15:11

May you know that "Joy to the World" includes you! He came to bring lasting joy to your life that the world can't take away. May joy be heard from your lips, expressed in your touch, and seen through your eyes. May joy be a choice you make in the easy and tough moments of this season so that strength will be your partner. May the good news that God brings you today cause great joy for you. May you see a bright light in any dark space as God's star shines for you. He wants you to rejoice with great joy! Joy packaged perfectly just for you has come. Receive this gift today and be exceedingly glad. May you hear Jesus speak to you and fill your joy. This is the day, this is the season, this is the time that the Lord has made. Rejoice and be glad in it!

354

Keep Praying

1 Thessalonians 5:17; Luke 18:1; Ephesians 6:18;
Psalm 40:1, 91:15, 116:2; Jeremiah 29:12

May you persist in prayer! May the discipline of prayer define your belief in what God can do. May you know that although your answers to prayer may not be revealed yet, God has heard you. He gets close and listens to you. Although it looks like your prayers may not have changed your situation in the time and way you had hoped, God is changing the way you experience each challenge, and He is changing you! Believe God for His perfect timing in your life. God hears the unspoken words of your heart. He receives the prayers you didn't even know you held. He receives you and will carry you. May you know that God is expecting you. He already plans to answer and honour you. Don't stop praying. God never fails!

355

Shift Your Focus

Matthew 19:26; 2 Corinthians 12:9; Luke 1:37;
2 Chronicles 20:15; John 14:27

May you walk into your strength because you continued to persevere through struggle. Every time you get back up, may you be empowered and encouraged by the truth that God's strength is made perfect in your weakness. May you and heaven laugh at all your "impossibilities" as God makes clear that all things are possible with Him. May you say that the battle is the Lord's and mean it. Stand still. Stand strong. Let Him take your stress and leave you with His peace. May you confidently worship instead of being committed to worry. Let God do His work. Trust God to do what is His to do in the first place. You focus on Him. May you look beyond where you are to where Jesus is going to take you. Don't get distracted. Only Jesus can see everything and everywhere. Focus on His power at work in you and for you. Focus on His love for you. Look up. Look forward. Look at Jesus.

356

Glory to God

Luke 2:11–14

May you understand the depth of the peace and goodwill that has come to you from the highest heaven and give all glory to God. May you be transformed in your heart and mind by the truth that the God of the universe thought of you and loved you so much that He came close to you. He came to you. He came for you. Sit with that and ponder the depth of love. Sit with Him and bask in His love. May you stand in awe of God's greatness and love. Both are limitless. Both carry miracle-working power. Both are for you. The angels are singing. Join them. There is much to sing about and celebrate.

357

All Is Calm

Matthew 1:23; John 1:14; Isaiah 9:6; Luke 1:38, 2:8–14

May all be calm and bright in your heart because Jesus has come. May all the busyness and chaos be stilled and dull in comparison to the hush, the sweet presence and light of God with us. May God visit you in a new way, and may you find things to be just as He has said as you search for new meaning and godly perspective in life's situations. May you experience a fresh anticipation and expectation that the peace and joy that has come will make a change. May you be certain that your hope is not in vain. Love has come to stay.

358

Know the Forever Christmas Truth

Luke 2:28–32; Joshua 1:9; Hebrews 13:8

May you be able to bless the Lord and remain in peace because of what the Lord has done from Christmas into all eternity. May you understand and receive the promises He has fulfilled and put into motion. May the light that God shines remove shadows from the spaces and places in your heart and bring needed revelation. May you move into new territory with boldness and courage, remembering that the Lord is with you and the hope, joy, love, and peace He brings is not just for a day or moment but for eternity. He is for your future. He is in your future. He is your future. Keep praising. Keep celebrating Him. He is the same God yesterday, today, and forever.

359

Happy Birthday, Jesus

Matthew 2:1–12

May you receive your king today with all your heart and have great joy! May you receive His presence that comes with overflowing love, ever-abiding peace, ever-filling joy, and everlasting hope as your most treasured gift this season. May He warm your heart today by ministering to the most intimate details of your life and meeting you exactly where you need Him. May today be a day of closeness with your Saviour. As you wish Him happy birthday, may you be even more aware of the gifts He gives. May you decide that He deserves more of you as you celebrate Him. He came to you willingly. May you come to Him. It will be the best gift you can give to yourself and Him.

360

Peace

Isaiah 9:6; Philippians 4:7; 2 Thessalonians 3:16; John 14:27

As you reflect on the baby born in a manger, may you experience His counsel and might and the protection of a Father. May the peace of God wash over you like never before. May the peace of God that passes all understanding fill your heart, home, and celebrations with the presence of God. May He be your most honoured guest in all you do. The Lord is with you. He will give you peace at all times. May you tangibly experience His peace on earth right where you are, and good will fall on you and be extended through you. The Lord freely gives His peace to you and leaves it with you. It is yours forever. Hold on to it and never let it go.

361

Hear Him Speak His Love

Psalm 17:8, 57:2, 103:17, 136:26; Zephaniah 3:17; 1 John 3:1;
Ephesians 2:10

May you hear God whisper His words of affection and love into your ear today. May you know that you are the apple of His eye and that He is looking on you with pride. May you be drawn into His loving embrace and stay there. You are His child, and He is honoured to call you His own. Let Him hold you. Let Him lift you. Let Him carry you.

Your Abba Father-Daddy will never leave you. He will never leave you alone. He will never leave you struggling. He will never leave you the way you are, as He has so much in store for you. He has big plans for you. You were created for a purpose. He will never leave you without His love. His love for you is everlasting.

362

Nothing Can Separate You

Romans 8:37–38; Psalm 139; John 3:16; Deuteronomy 7:9;
1 John 4:9–11

May you know that there is nothing you have done, are doing, or ever will do that will separate you from the love of God. His love reaches you wherever you are. When you sit and rise, in the dark or in the light, His love calls you. His love hears you. His love is for you. He made you who you are and loves you that way. You are fearfully and wonderfully made. You are unique and uniquely loved. There is only one you. The one and only God loves the one and only you.

Remember this truth: God so loved you that His Son died for you so that you can live in love. God keeps His covenant of love with you. Grow in His love as you keep His commands, and know that God remains faithful in His love to you for generations to come. God loved you first, loves you still, and will love you last. You are forever loved.

363

His Great Love

John 15:9, 13; 1 John 4:8; Jude 1:21; Ephesians 3:17–19; Isaiah 54:10

Today may you believe with all your heart that there is no greater love for you than the love of God. He has laid down His life for you in great love for you. May you allow His great love for you to build your courage and erase fear. You can be bold in His love. His perfect love casts out all your fears. When you are afraid, remember He loves you. When you have doubt, remember He loves you. When the enemy comes to lie to you and fill you with guilt, remember He loves you and you are forgiven.

Keep yourself in the love of God. Remember that the devil is always a liar, and God is always truth. Abide in Him and His love. May you be rooted and grounded in His love and grow to understand the breadth, length, height, and depth of His love for you. May His love fill your every thought and every space in your heart. Things and people will come and go in your life, but God's steadfast love will always be with you.

364

Bear Fruit in His Love

Psalm 52:8; 1 Peter 4:8; Matthew 22:37–39; 2 Thessalonians 3:5; Lamentations 3:22–23; John 13:34–35; 1 Corinthians 13:4–8

As you continue to trust in the steadfast love of the Lord today, may you be like an olive tree that produces continually for the glory of God. May you always know how much you are loved and love yourself that deeply so that you can love others freely. Keep loving others with the love you have received from God. Your love will be a blessing and cover over a multitude of sins. As you love the Lord your God with all your heart, soul, and mind, may you continually be filled with His love to love your neighbour as yourself. God loves to use you to show His love.

May the Lord direct your heart to His love and keep you steadfast in Christ. As you stay in Him, you will bear much fruit. May you experience a new expression of God's love for you today and every day. His steadfast love never ceases and is new every morning. May you find joy in God's love and how His love overflows to others through you. He loves you so much. Love others as He has loved you. Let your love be the testimony that you are a child of God. His love is the greatest and will never end.

365

Stay with Him

Isaiah 49:16, 58:11; Psalm 139:10; Proverbs 3:5–6; John 15:5;
Jeremiah 17:7–8; Luke 12:32

May you decide today that whatever comes in your future, you will stay with God. May you decide that your future is in the best hands and hold His hands tightly. May every situation that you don't understand lead you to trust God's heart even more. God always has a plan. May your roots go deep in God. Stay rooted because it promises blessings. Keep your roots in the one who is faithful in making sure you bear fruit. May hope for your future be rooted in God and the promises He has already fulfilled. The Lord has already been your guide, and He will not stop. You are worth too much to Him. He has so much to give you. Trust your today and your tomorrow to the one who created everything for you to enjoy. Stay with Him and enjoy the surprises He has for you!

ABOUT THE AUTHOR

Shireen Spencer is a gifted preacher and motivational speaker who loves to share her story of what God has done through her struggles to encourage and bring healing to others suffering the same challenges and heartaches. She is a pastor, an associate with Family Life Canada, an elementary school teacher, and a Mary Kay business owner. She's also a fully trained, equipped, and licensed officiant, life celebration professional, and certified life coach. She's been described as friendly, gregarious, and passionate about bringing out the best in people. She's married to the love of her life, Che Spencer, and together they have two wonderful boys. They currently reside in the Greater Toronto Area.

Shireen is also the author of *Big Challenges, Even Bigger God: Finding God Faithful in the Hard Moments of Life* (2019) and *I Still Say, I Do: Keeping your Marriage Vows Alive through the Seasons and the Storms* (2020 with Che Spencer).

Big Challenges, Even Bigger GOD

Finding God
Faithful in the Hard
Moments of Life

Shireen Spencer

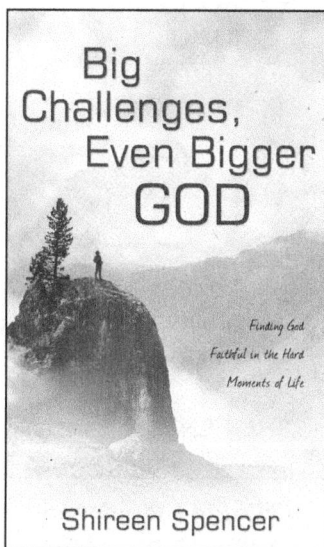

ISBN: 978-1-4866-1805-7

"Shireen shares her story with transparency and explores every moment in which she faced overwhelming trials. Her determination to walk through fires with faith is deeply inspiring. God's fingerprints and the evidence of His presence in these moments are explicit."
—Cyndi Desjardins Wilkens, Author of *Shine On*

Sometimes life feels like it's just a constant series of trials, each season presenting us with a new challenge to work through. What do we do in times when things are going from bad to worse? Is it possible to still live in joy and see God at work in our lives?

In *Big Challenges... Even Bigger God!*, Shireen Spencer shows that it is, sharing her own hard-learned understanding that, while life is hard, *God is good*.

You too can live every day in the knowledge that this is true. That even when you fear that you are alone, and feel that He has left you, God is always at work in your life. Remember, the challenges that we face in life may be big, but God is bigger! It's time for everyone to experience the comfort of God's presence in even the darkest of times.

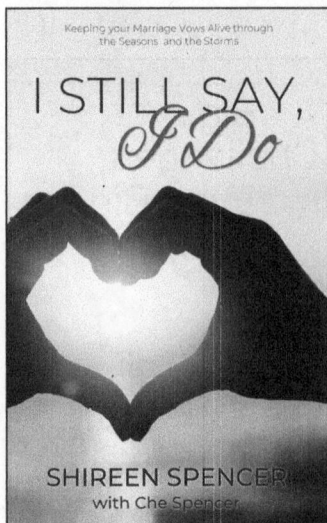

ISBN: 978-1-4866-1809-5

"You will love the passion, authenticity, and vulnerability of Shireen and Che Spencer in this helpful book. Don't miss out on their grounded and practical message."
—Drs. Les and Leslie Parrott, #1 New York Times-bestselling authors of *Saving Your Marriage Before It Starts*

On the day we get married, life looks perfect. Our vows are said with such conviction and promise. Then life hits and the storms come and our wedding day can seem like a distant memory.

Sharing their own story of difficulty and coming face to face with the reality of each vow, Che and Shireen Spencer share how their dependence on God kept them saying "I do" through each season of marriage. With God on their side, their marriage was made stronger. Just as strongly as they repeated the words "I do" on a beautiful June day years ago, they still say "I do" today—and you can too!